# Land of the Exiles
## A Silent Eye Workbook with Practical Notes
### Steve Tanham

The Hawk has crash-landed on the planet Idos, the crew awake from cryogenic sleep to find that their captain is missing and the ship has been taken over by a cyborg who bends them to his will, making them play out the stories of the ancient gods of Egypt as it seeks to understand what it is to be human. Their only hope of survival lies in the strange touch of the Mindstream, and their own inner hearts.

Land of the Exiles is a practical and teaching guide to a fully scripted ritual workshop from the Silent Eye, a modern Mystery School.

With contributions from Sue Vincent, Stuart France and some of the Companions of the Hawk… those who shared the ritual… who give a glimpse of how such a workshop *really* works.

Published by Silent Eye Press


The Silent Eye School of Consciousness
ISBN-13: 978-1910478011
ISBN-10: 1910478016

# Land of the Exiles

## A Silent Eye Workbook with Practical Notes

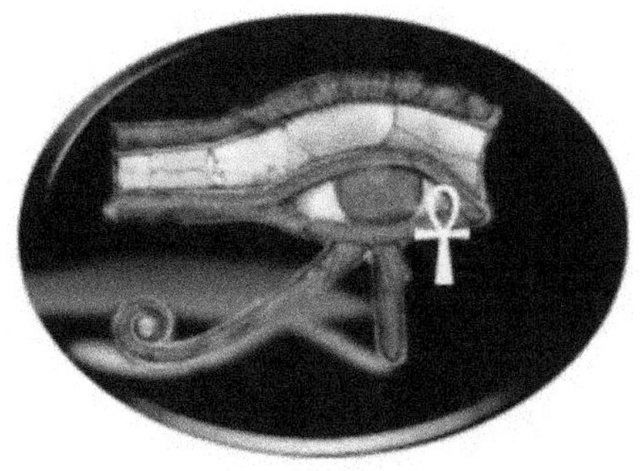

## Steve Tanham

with

### Sue Vincent, Stuart France
### & the Companions of the Hawk

To Sue and Stuart, Companions of the Rose and the Soul
. . . and the fall hasn't killed us yet!

# Contents

# A letter from Sheila

**Sheila Chadwick**
*Bast*

Dear Steve, Sue and Stuart

I will attempt to put into words my feelings about the weekend.
Here goes.
Excitement was in the air, meeting old and new friends.
The anniversary of the birthing of the new school, anticipation regarding the Rituals.
I was playing the role of Bast, the Egyptian Goddess of joy, twin sister of Horus. The atmosphere in the temple over the weekend built up to a dramatic climax, it felt like a crucible which attracted the release of essence.
We had enjoyable talks from Steve, lots of laughter which for me is so stimulating, going with the flow, opening the heart to the message of the Silent Eye teachings.
The memories linger on afterwards, learning through play, humour, and above all companionship.

Love & Light,
Sheila x

# Foreword

**Sue Vincent**
*Isis*

There were hugs. Lots of them, as people began to arrive in the 'Land of the Exiles' for the Silent Eye weekend workshop. There was a moment when I had armfuls of people it seemed... several at once... then singly... then together. It is good to greet old friends and the work we do builds a sympathetic bond. A few are students of the School, but most had simply come from across the world, some thousands of miles, to join us for the weekend. The workshops are open to all, a place and time to share views, thoughts, insight and ideas. It was wonderful to greet old friends from SOL (the Servants of the Light) with whom we three had shared a path through the Western Mystery Tradition, but this was not the only tradition by any manner of means... Christian and Shaman, energy-worker and Daoist, Wiccan and Qabalist, to name but a few... came together to explore the concepts raised in the shape of a rather odd ritual drama.

Except, of course, by definition drama can be as *apparently* odd as it likes; it doesn't have to be 'real' in terms of historical fact in order to be real. It is a story... a symbolic journey... sometimes an analogy, sometimes an illustration of another level of understanding. The concept worked and allowed us to meld the ancient and the futuristic to create a frame for the spiritual journey we were about to share. These things affect each participant differently but they are always an intense and emotional experience.

By four o'clock Friday my little room at the Nightingale Centre was strewn with robes and costumes. The Temple space had been constructed, the candles placed. A backdrop had begun to take shape... a spontaneous using of things to hand to create the physical and visible form of sacred space, in the same way that the costumes create an open doorway into imagination. We keep it simple.

Outside the pages of occult fiction these things *of themselves* hold no meaning. In a hallowed space where people work together from the heart and with intent, they take on a different feel, touching the emotions and circumventing the need for intellectualised explanations. Like a child with a picture book, these things simply speak to the imagination and the heart. Yet there is more to it. Photographs cannot, do not, capture sacred intent, the hushed atmosphere, the reverence and respect for the Life behind life.

The first evening is fairly gentle, setting the scene and allowing everyone to find their feet. There was a welcome, an explanation of what we were going to share… time to settle in and meet each other, as old friends or new. The Temple was consecrated with Light, then the first drama began as white robed sleepers were woken on the deck of a space ship. The captain was missing and in his place a robot… a cyborg who worked with logic alone and who had chosen to explore the difference between his own mechanical life and that of humanity. The flashing green diodes reinforced the gap between the two modes of being… the laser that controlled and coerced was a direct contrast to the gentle illumination of the central flame. Setaxa chose his victim… holding her hostage against our compliance as he imposed his will and cast the crew as ancient gods, to play out their story that he might understand his own….

After which, it seemed a little light refreshment was in order and most of us repaired to the Queen Anne next door to relax and enjoy the laughter. Outside the moon approached the full and glancing up we saw a very odd phenomenon… a clear ring around the bright face… like a giant eye in the heavens, ever widening. We took it as a hopeful sign that the coming day would hold something special.

We were right…

*Sue Vincent*
*Director – The Silent Eye*
*2014*

# A Calling...

**Benjamin Prewitt**
*Technician*

There comes a time in each of our lives when we here a calling, a drive or passion that takes us to the next level or starts us on a path of self discovery that is impossible to ignore. Over the past few years I've had the pleasure and honour of travelling to the Great Buxton Hollow and cradling myself into Derbyshire amongst some of the most passionate, committed and wise people I've met in my life.

Attending the second annual School of the Silent Eye seminar is, and forever will be, one of the more profound journeys my life has taken me on. The first year and Christening of the school sent us all on a path of discovery, strength and temperance. The second for me has helped provide the insight I've needed to navigate some of the most treacherous waters my life has come to know.

Never in my life have I experienced the wisdom and true soulful gathering as I have with the School of the Silent Eye. I'm forever joined and forever thankful.

Namaste
Benjamin M Prewitt.
2014

# Introduction

## Sunglasses, Spaceships and Rituals on Idos

As our involvement with the world increases, we forget where we came from. Not biologically, but where our sense of "myself" came from. Most of this sense of self crystallised in our childhood - typically before the age of seven.

The vividness of childhood is often remembered as flashes of a life in which we were in immediate contact with our experience of the world, in all its fullness. The gradual loss of this, often described later in life as a progressive numbing, is taken to be inevitable in the process of growing up. Big boys and girls don't cry - although, of course, we do, and often the most painful thing in our adult lives is that nebulous memory of what and who we once were, in those bright and shining days, when every breath involved our whole being.

This process of separation from our essential selves is not random. Over the past century, Psychology has provided a scientific rationale for what mysticism and magic have taught for millennia. But Psychology aims at a more polished version of our "outer self" - a more balanced personality, to use familiar terminology. Freud gave us the word "ego". It was a powerful attempt to define the self we seek to build as we struggle with maturity in our lives. From this perspective, the psyche contains different divisions. The lowest foundation of this is the "id", a powerful reservoir of our wilder, more childlike and often fiery passions - but which is nonetheless the source of the energy of our selves. High above this, but in the societal and moral sense only, is the "Superego". The Superego is a living process of behaviour correction, accompanied by an image of one or more of our parental figures, or a similar authority figure from those early days. In the presence of our Superego, we can feel ourselves shrinking, as we become a child again, in the face of a force we must obey. Any form of dictatorship forces us back into dealing with the Superego, which is why dictators can have such a negative effect on our sense of self. We are, literally, crushed - made smaller.

Between the wild but largely caged id and the superego, we try to live in a balanced structure known simply as our "ego". This home of the regular self is the one psychologists attempt to stabilise in the case of mental illness. Most of us are blessed with mental stability, but the above descript

-tions can often help us be more sympathetic with those who are not.

From the perspective of this ego defined like this, we came to be here in three stages. We were born from a world inside Mother, to a world separated but still close to Mother. Our naked self, in all the senses of the word, faced the fear of the unknown beyond Mother - a place it had to go into in order to establish its own identity, which was a hunger almost as powerful as the need for breath and food. Finally, we found that those immediately around us, starting with Mother, couldn't always reflect back to us what we needed, in terms of our hunger for identity. At a certain point, we separated ourselves, in a fundamental sense, and took the first steps to becoming an individual.

Looked at in this way, our whole life journey has been one of the creation of that individual. So-called winners are always strong individuals. Kindness is often considered to have no place in this level of success, though previous ages might have considered things differently. The cost is the separation of our original, and very powerful self, what the Silent Eye School refers to as Essence, from the structure of the personality in which we now live. The personality lives by reacting to things in our lives as they appear in our field of consciousness, with its five windows of sensory experience and the vast capacity to form an internal world to deal with how our beliefs tell us it should all fit together.

The whole of this is a necessary and not a negative thing. From a spiritual perspective, we have to become an individual before we can become something else. That something else is a step that few people take, but it is the essence of the spiritual journey. However you conceive of your creator, whether in an anthropomorphic or discarnate sense, the journey back to the source is powered by the fuel that the ego has become. In some ways it involves its dissolution; but this should be viewed as analogous to the lifecycle of the butterfly rather than that of a destructive process. The artificial mental and emotional structure of the ego must be slowly dissolved into a clear liquid of potential, if the life of our essence, our spirit, is to be realised. Then the inner architect can be given free rein to re-model us to become our brighter selves, and even beyond that, into something else entirely.

All the major paths teach this. They may not expose the beginner to such forthright language at the start of the journey, but, ultimately, they have to. The ego has been cast as the villain in many traditions, but really it is not. It is a necessary stage in the lifecycle of the soul. What matters most is the recognition and acceptance of that "tap on the shoulder" from within to say that the time is right and that we had better be about it, if this lifetime and this personality, is to become the vehicle of spiritual transition.

Symbolic systems can help us in grasping all of this, and in a way that opens the power of the emotions as well as that of the intellect. This is essential if we are to sustain that initial enthusiasm. The world of modern magic, known mainly under the banner of the Western Mystery Tradition, uses a derivation of the Hebrew Tree of Life. This structure of ten-plus-one "spheres" and their corresponding twenty-two paths are the subject of a very detailed and often intellectually focused attribution of both principles of objective knowledge and the subjective journey one takes, as the individual moves their personal focus from the body-centric experiences of ordinary life to the more abstract views of the soul.

The Tree of Life, in its Qabalistic settings was created long before the advent of modern psychology and therefore does not benefit from the past hundred years of deep investigation into the process of "how me-ness develops in our world". Many will argue that this is not necessary, and that getting beyond this is the important thing. There is certainly truth in that, but the biggest obstacles to that progress are the forces of the personality/ego itself. These have evolved to a definite shape in each of our lives. None of us are the same, but the primal experiences of coming into life had exactly the same elements. The different results - we - are the product of the reactions to those forces, which are still very much present in our lives, although mainly invisible. The word for invisible in this field of study is subconscious. The subconscious is nothing more than the sinking of what was once conscious - a daily reality - below the horizon of what is noticed. For these reasons a new approach to the journey towards our essential and therefore spiritual nature has been pioneered during the time that psychology has been maturing. This branch of self-development is often called "spiritual psychology", and one offshoot of it uses a very powerful symbol called the Enneagram.

The modern enneagram is a symbol of relationship, unfolding and personality. Not all these elements came together at the same time. The original enneagram was brought to the West by G.I. Gurdjieff in the early years of the last century. This remarkable man, an Armenian mystic who said he had (eventually) been schooled by a mysterious group of spiritual guides called the Sarmoun Brotherhood in central Asia, was the creator of what became known as the Fourth Way. Among his foremost students (from an English perspective) were P. D. Ouspensky, Maurice Nicoll and John Bennett. The Fourth Way offers a direct and very focused path to self-development, but it is difficult to find a school with the same vibrancy as that which accompanied its birth in Moscow around 1912, and the forty years that followed.

The Enneagram is discussed in detail in the sections of this book, but in the context of the Ritual Dramas which form its core. For now, let us continue to set the scene as to its use in the esoteric psychology movement and the latter's adoption as teaching basis by the Silent Eye School.

Not all users of the modern enneagram are concerned with spiritual development. Many are focused on the personality and the strengthening of it for use in "normal" life. Gurdjieff did not teach the use of the enneagram for such purposes, but he did place a great deal of emphasis on dealing with the personality and was often seen, humorously and some would say, brutally, demonstrating the latter's inconsistencies. His jocular after-dinner games about "the twenty-one Idiots" and each person's "Chief Feature" - the one outstandingly negative trait to which we are all individually blind - became one of his trademarks. There was no cruelty in this. He had set himself to use the technique of what he called "shocks" as an effective teaching tool, though it was not always received that way, as personality did what it does best, and took offence, thereby cutting the soul off from the jewels of deeper awareness that were present in each of such encounters.

Gurdjieff cared little for what the world thought of him. He had set his life's work to be the exposition of a clear, personal path to the individual essence, the restoration of that living link with the young soul within us all, the part of us that never lost the connection with its home. He knew this could not be achieved without struggle, so he did his best to equip those he helped to deal with the inner struggle - the greater part of which was against the entrenched view of self-contained in the personality. In this he was one of the foremost advocates of restoring the proximity of that link to the Divine within our selves. No priests were necessary with the Fourth Way - a tradition that has continued within those Schools that have derived, in some form at least, from the powerful approaches that Gurdjieff left us.

The Silent Eye is such a school, although it is not one that is entirely in the Fourth Way tradition. Founded on the principle that it would be possible to combine elements of the Western Mystery Tradition with the dramatic advances in esoteric psychology, our early experiences opened possibilities to us in the form of an individual approach which combined magical pathworking (guided meditations) with the use of the spiritual enneagram. One of the techniques we brought with us into the Silent Eye was the use of what the Greeks would have called "Mystery Plays", derived from our extensive experience of using ritual drama within Dolores Ashcroft-Nowicki's Servants of the Light organisation, a School in the Western Mystery Tradition. We have tried to push the boundaries of this noble art to embrace a whole new frontier of what can be considered "sacred". The ostensibly sci-fi basis of the 2014 workshop is just one example of this. The monthly lessons of the Silent Eye course are another example of a radical and vivid departure from the normal process of esoteric teaching.

Before you is an unusual book. It is partly a transcript of the contiguous ritual dramas of the annual Silent Eye Workshop, held in the middle of beautiful Derbyshire in the spring of 2014, and called The Land of the Exiles. This is augmented by the addition of explanatory chapters to accompany each act in the unfolding story. People turned up from across the globe to play their parts in bringing this to life. Some were experienced ritualists, but several were there for the first time. Everyone had a great weekend and took away moments they will never forget. Many of the testimonials attest to this, and to the fun we all had doing it.

The Divine loves you, and is as personal as it is universal. It is everywhere in your life. It lives between your heartbeats and in the silences in which thought is not the dominant presence. It is witness to all your struggles and also your achievements. Find it and be with it. Love it and be open to its effects. Then, be silent and watch what happens in your life.

Have fun - we did!


## The Play, Playing and the Players

Consider the word 'Play'. What comes to mind?

For most of us, it will be a picture of a theatrical production. We will imagine a bustle of people moving slowly into a theatre to watch a popular production. The audience will be well-behaved, respectful and attuned to the players in front of them on the stage. There will be a consciousness of decorum, of the necessary confines and limitations of a story told within a restricted space. Those more familiar with theatre will know that such confinement produces an experience somehow greater because of the nature and intensity of the personal relationship between audience and players in such a limited arena.

From a physical perspective, the audience will be passive. Their role is to sit, quietly and absorb. The players will be active. Their role is to work with each other, and the unspoken sensitivities of the audience, to convey the deepest meaning held in the words of the script. When this works well, there is an incomparable presence in the theatre. Something ancient in the human psyche is working. There comes a sense of a different experience, a level of sharing something that goes way beyond everyday life. The trivial drops away as the spoken word becomes the conveyer of *meaning*.

Simplicity and beauty, combine on a stage to produce something entirely different from, say, a film.

Theatre is as old as mankind. Few people speak of ritual in the same breath, and yet the birth of both ritual and theatre - the play, are likely to have entered our collective consciousness at the same time. Humankind loves a story. To share in its telling seems to touch us at the most profound level.

The Greeks gave us a substantial history of the world as it was then. Pythagoras spoke, not only of his own world, but also the world of the Egyptian Mystery Schools in which he studied for many years. Initiations carried out by the Egyptian priesthood were deliberately mysterious, and designed to produce heightened, emotional states of consciousness, in which the right seed-thoughts could be planted to bear fruit, either immediately, if the candidate was ready, or later in the candidate's life, if he or she was not.

This principle of theatre as initiatory space remains with us today in modern Mystery Schools, particularly in the West. There is something deeply 'opening' about being part of a staged production. It is very liberating when it goes well. There is also the risk of it being a poor experience if it goes badly.

Yet, few people think of the other, and much more common meaning of the word 'Play'. Literally, to do as children do, and explore by Playing. Built into the development of our brains, this principle hides a deeply serious purpose - to come to terms with the world as it really is - Objective Reality, learned by fun, trial and error. We do not often think about the juxtaposition of the two meanings of Play. Yet they are deeply entwined in the human soul. To learn by doing, with fun and without fear, is a natural process within our minds.

A normal theatre production takes a well-rehearsed cast and an appropriate stage. Given the vast range of styles, there are few rules, but that appropriateness is everything. As in life, the overly ornate will lose out to the simple when it comes to that passage of meaning from object to viewer, given the right script . . .

What happens if you take away the time to rehearse? In a staged production, you would get a state of panic, with the more experienced actors being able to cope, and the less experienced being less able to manage the shift towards the edge of chaos. But what if you wanted that edge of chaos to prevail, to transform itself into something very different? What happens if you reduce the rehearsal time to zero?

In the Silent Eye School, we are pioneering a new type of Ritual Drama. In our major workshops, we work with a different type of Play - a single story which spans a whole weekend. The various Acts within that play will divide the action into its major stages, with the first Act being a relatively gentle introduction to the major theme of the weekend, but told, in role, by the whole cast. By the middle of the weekend the tension will be high, with elements of opposition at the peak of their power. By the final Act, on the Sunday morning, there comes a longing for all the stretched threads to be pulled together; for the Alchemy of Transformation to work its magic, bringing the improbable into the *now* in an act of super-physical, psychological healing whose function is to create a gateway through which all the participants pass - an initiation, in its truest sense. For the players, the performers (and we are all performers at these events), it can be a life-changing moment. As the production team, our job is to ensure it is - and many years of getting it right speak for our record in this.

And the audience? Well, there isn't one, because we are all Players in this . . .

And yet, in a much deeper sense, there is, because we all receive the shared experience. The most spiritually attuned will see the unfolding of the story on a deeper level. Those new to it will gain from simply being part of the outer story, but will feel the pull of the inner story, too. We have all made this progression, and we look to nurture those new to it.

In any of the main workshops from the Silent Eye School, we all play a character, a role. Someone playing, say, a Priest in the Temple of Isis - one of the main characters in The River of the Sun, our spring 2015 workshop, will hold the same role throughout the weekend. By doing this, the players come to hold the "spirit" of the part - and are therefore changed by it.

It may sound daunting, but it is not, and it is the reason that people come back year after year to try the next gateway of the developing Self.

We have a very brief walk through for each Act; but this simply covers the actual movements in the temple/theatre space. Handbooks containing the full scripts are published well before the weekend and distributed as PDFs, allowing ample time to become familiar with the nominated part. We read the parts from the scripts as though doing a final, script-assisted, rehearsal. You may think that this limits things, but, we can assure you it does not. The creative tension and participation, the sheer joy of being part of a work of shared creation unfolding before you, is something you will never forget.

Come and join us for the next one, you might like it!

## How to use this book

There are many ways you can use this book. It contains a complete transcript of the workshop, with the full parts of all the characters.

*Option 1*- You could simply read it. There is a considerable amount of knowledge expressed in the words of each of the characters. The sections that follow will show you what to look for. The drama is set within a temple layout. This is the actual temple arrangement used by the Silent Eye School for its own rituals. The power and focus of the different parts of the temple structure are brought out at various points in the ritual dramas. The early dramas use a simple variant of this, but the action gets more complex as the story unfolds - bringing in more of the available power as a well-executed ritual always does. The power of the 'group mind' of such a gathering is quite something. This power also grows through the course of the weekend as involvement deepens.

You may think that this is not available to the present reader, after the event. However, a magical ritual once enacted remains in a state of accessible manifestation and is available to anyone who seeks it out with sincere purpose. Try it and see!

*Option 2* - You could assume one of the parts and imagine the dramas unfolding with you as an active participant. Much rests on the magician's art of active imagination. Do you have it? Trying out one or more of these dramas is one way of finding out and developing this esoteric skill - in fact, it is one of the best routes you can take, because the story will involve you.

The more you get into it, the more will your powerful imagination work for you. Imagination takes two forms: there is idle imagination, which is just daydreaming - relaxing and restful in itself, but lacking power for transformative action. Then there is active imagination, where the constructed scene is used as a canvas, a mental and emotional screen on which our inner self can project important elements of learning or revelation, based on the seeds sown in us by the rituals.

A full list of parts is given in the appendix and as part of the introduction to the next chapter.

You could act out a part in your head, or by walking around and imagining you are there. You could swap the role selected and see the action from differing perspectives. You could even mark out the temple design - shown in the book before each ritual drama, in miniature, and enact some or all of the movements. Movement is one of the key techniques that generates magical power in a temple. This simple truth has profound implications that can be used, even in a small home temple or altar space.

*Option 3* - You could share the book with others, using a small group to read out selected parts or to rotate speakers, such that each person simply takes the next spoken paragraph. We use this technique when we first write the ritual dramas, to test for the effect and the feel of it coming from different voices. This is a very effective way of working with these scripts.

## The General Arrangement of the Parts

The plot is set on a stage whose layout is the control deck (the *Bridge*) of the Hawk, the colonising spaceship which has been deliberately crash-landed on the destination planet of Idos. This 'space' is the setting for all the Acts of the weekend's story. Such a space is limited, of necessity. This act of limitation is a part of all temple working, and reflects a deep esoteric principle - that the Universe (and any act of creation) comes into existence through a deliberate act of limitation and division by a creative force that gives it birth. This is the origin of the 'magical circle' - a space circumscribed by the magician, whose purpose is to achieve a specific goal. In the Land of the Exiles, the space is the temple, which is the control deck of the spaceship. The specific goal is to use the confinement so generated to force a process of human alchemy. The effect - in the play and with the actual players working the parts - is to bring out the best of what is truly human, against the counterpoint of an apparently hostile machine - the Hawk's computer/

cyborg, whose real nature is gradually revealed as the story progresses.

The parts are divided into three groups, reflecting the physical layout of the temple/bridge of the Hawk. The reader is referred to the generic temple diagram at the start of Ritual Drama 1.

# One of the best

**Chris Hutchinson**
*Sia*

I was a newcomer to The Silent Eye and thus inevitably cautious about joining a bunch of people for a weekend in the fabulous vistas of The Nightingale Centre near Buxton. The experience from start to finish left me feeling completely safe, loved, and stimulated. I had old thinking challenged, new thinking introduced and, woven through a gripping drama, taken on a fascinating journey alongside my new friends 'The Companions'. In the past I have been immersed in many group experiences, residential or otherwise, and this ranks as one of the best!

# A Welcome Bridge

**Trine Moore**
*Thoth*

Transformations, those surely happen, and the setting helps. A quiet village, great people and community, and pheasants and owls... That's real nightlife!

We met as a company of souls, we are worldwide. People travel to attend the annual event of Silent Eye. There's a story, we each have a part to play, a role within our Passion Play, newcomers there are, and welcomes abound. This year was the birthday of the Silent Eye; bridging ancient truths with science's discoveries... It's a great opportunity to become, in a great environment. And a Welcome Bridge in turbulent times.

## Chapter One
# The Big Picture

It will be useful to the reader to have, at the start of each Ritual Drama, an overview of the relevant part of the plot. The value of the workshop is in the personal alchemy of how the changes happen within the group performing it, rather than simply knowing what happens. We also show, here, the general layout of the temple space and the roles used within it. The roles evolve from an initial set of ship's officers to an enforced playing of Egyptian Gods and Goddesses. The background for this is revealed by the drama, which follows.

Each subsequent chapter will build on this, showing the symbolic and developmental basis of the workshop's unfolding.

The story is of a group of space colonists whose ship, The Hawk, has crash-landed on their destination planet – Idos. They know nothing of this until they are awakened from their cryogenic sleep by the ship's computer – or rather, the cyborg, which operates as a mobile extension of the central computer. His name is Setaxa (SElf TAsking eXecutive Automaton), and he provides the antagonistic force in the dramas, as spaceship computers often do. But this plot is subtly different. The entire story is really about the redemption of this semi-mechanical intelligence at the hands of the very people he comes to terrorise. There are, obviously, very deep undertones to this and it draws many parallels with a wealth of esoteric literature.

### Ritual Drama 1 – The story

For the seven years prior to the crash-landing – which Setaxa himself engineers so that the ship will be crippled and the crew kept under his control – the cyborg has enjoyed a deep mental relationship with the ship's Captain, who was the only human awake during the long voyage. The Captain is also a cybernetics expert, and deliberately engineered this interstellar period – despite the risks to his own health of staying awake – in order to bring the new generation cyborg to an advanced state of man-machine hybrid consciousness. When the story begins, the Captain is missing and the cyborg has assumed his identity and morphed into a simulacrum of him. The newly-awakened crew immediately suspect that the Captain is being impersonated, but tread carefully following the revelation by the unmasked cyborg that he has surgically engineered pain/pleasure implants into their nervous systems, allowing him to control or reward them using his laser "wand".

When it is revealed by Setaxa that the Captain is actually missing, the crew immediately suspect the cyborg. He protests his innocence, eventually stating that the missing Captain was his only friend. Despite this insight into his kinder side, the cyborg maintains his iron grip on the mission, judging himself to be the only one capable of carrying out the Captain's last instructions, which he will not reveal. The story, therefore, begins in antagonism, and stays that way as an intellectual and, eventually, emotional confrontation is played out, at increasingly deeper levels and with escalating risks for the crew.

## Temple layout and associated roles

The temple layout is closely related to the roles in the drama. See Figure 1.

The main elements of the temple layout are as follows:

The temple consists of a series of three circles set within a square. The square represents the standard magical temple layout, with sides of East, West, North and South. Entry to the temple room is via the West and then, usually, clockwise around the temple, though Setaxa openly breaks this convention. Later in the rituals dramas, the Rings assume opposite rotations. During the weekend, this had a very powerful magical effect, and marked a vivid turning point in the energy levels operating in the temple space.

The heart of the Silent Eye temple space is the Enneagram. This nine-pointed figure will be discussed in the next chapter.

The core enneagram figure is surrounded by two circles. From inner to outer, representing the flow of spiritual light outwards from the centre. They are the Ring of Bright and the Ring of Shadows. Both of the rings share nine positions, which project, radially, from the nine points on the enneagram.

## Land of the Exiles
## Generic Temple Diagram

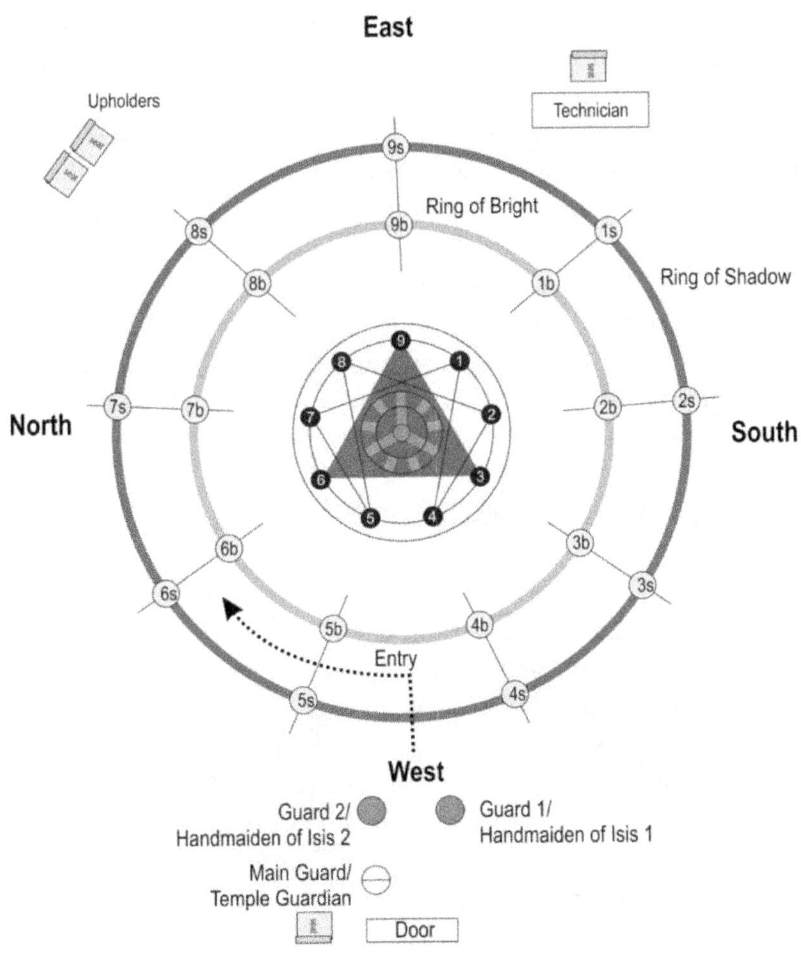


*Figure 1 - the standard temple layout, representing the Bridge of the Hawk*

The heart of the temple, the symbolic chalice and flame, are placed in the exact centre.

The entrance stations in the West are for the Temple Guardian, who begins the workshop as a kind of head of security; and two secondary guards, who become the Handmaidens of Isis later in the workings.

The entire East (see photographs p.41 and p.106) is dedicated to the power of the figure of Isis, who begins the workshop as the First Officer and is then forced by Setaxa to assume the female lead role.

There is a table for the technician who has a key role in ensuring that the music and sound files get played at the right point in each ritual. Music includes entrance and exit pieces, plus themed music clips designed to give an emotional link to key elements, such as the communications from the Mindstream – a discarnate intelligence native to Idos, which is intent on helping the colonists on the ship.

Any upholders (those without a named part who have an important role in maintaining the purposeful atmosphere in the temple space) are seated in the Northeast, as shown.

## The Roles used in the Workshop

The roles played within this space are shown in Figure 2, below, and are based initially on nine functions of the ship's officers. The positions taken are either followed by the letter 'b' or 's'. These relate to the Rings of Bright (b) and Shadow (s). The officer functions, e.g. *Intelligence*, are mirrored within the same radial line. So, for example, position 5b and 5s are linked, radially, with the point 5 on the inner figure – the enneagram. Point 5b is initially the primary Intelligence Officer, denoted with a '1' as in "Intelligence Officer 1". The second Intelligence officer (Intelligence Officer 2) occupies position 5s. As Ritual Drama 1 unfolds, you will see how for example, the primary Intelligence Officer is cast by Setaxa as Anubis. In similar fashion, the secondary Intelligence Officer becomes Neith. All other characters follow the same model, with the exception of the First Officer (Isis) and the Exploration Officer (Horus). These two characters, central to the action in the story, occupy both the positions in the Rings of Bright and Shadow.

From the first ritual on, the roles are entirely based on the Egyptian archetypes. There are occasional references to the former functions, as appropriate to what Setaxa is trying to achieve in his doomed quest to run humans as machines.

## So, what's really going on?

Setaxa, the cyborg extension of the ship's computer, has a name that clearly links him to the Egyptian figure of Set. Set has many attributes, but within this workshop, we use him as a representation of the *ego*. The ego is that part of us that has the sense of 'me-ness'. It grows with us through life, although it is largely formed by the age of seven. It is composed entirely of *reactions*. Later in life it gets cleverer and more manipulative. It believes itself to be the only one that can run the ship of ourselves – but it is, as Gurdjieff said, a *machine*. It is a machine because it, and our sense of self, is based upon the story of our lives as stored in our brains. As such, it belongs entirely to the physical world – the world of Becoming. The other world, the world we came from at birth, is the world of Being and the home of our true and suppressed self. The radical differences between these two worlds are the subtext of the Land of the Exiles. The ego is discussed, in context, in more detail, in the chapters that follow.

For now, if you're ready, read the first Ritual Drama and feel your way in! Select a role and live it. Enjoy!

# Roles and Positions in the Temple

**Initial Positions**

*Ring of Bright*

1b - Navigation Officer 1 (Nut)
2b- Medical Officer 1 (Nephthys)
3b - Exploration Officer 1 (Horus)
4b - Conformance Officer 1 (Shu)
5b - Intelligence Officer 1 (Anubis)
6b - Defence Officer 1 (Sekhmet)
7b - Planning Officer 1 (Thoth)
8b - Weapons Officer 1 (Geb)
9b - First Officer (Isis)

**Initial Positions**

*Ring of Shadows*

1s - Navigation Officer 2 (Maat)
2s- Medical Officer 2 (Hathor)
3s - Exploration Officer 2 (None)
4s - Conformance Officer 2 (Tefnut)
5s - Intelligence Officer 2 (Neith)
6s - Defence Officer 2 (Setaxa)
7s - Planning Officer 2 (Sia)
8s - Weapons Officer 2 (Bast)
9b - None (First Officer/Isis occupies both inner and outer positions as her wings encompass the whole temple)

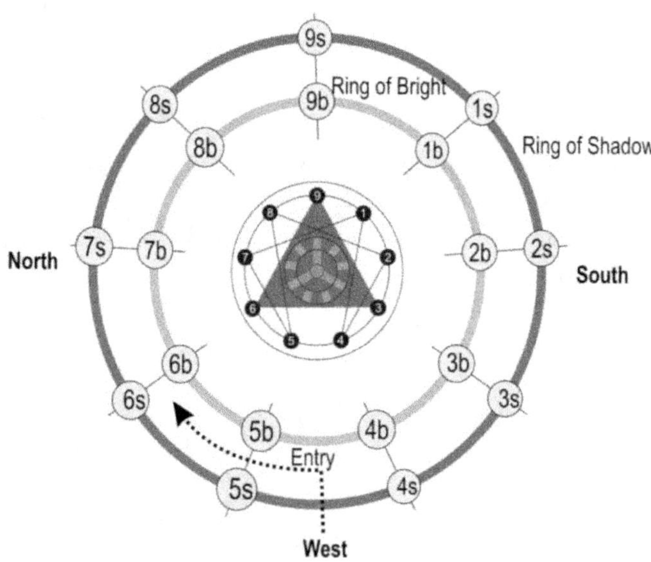


*Figure 2 - The Roles for the Workshop*

# Ritual One
# Arrival

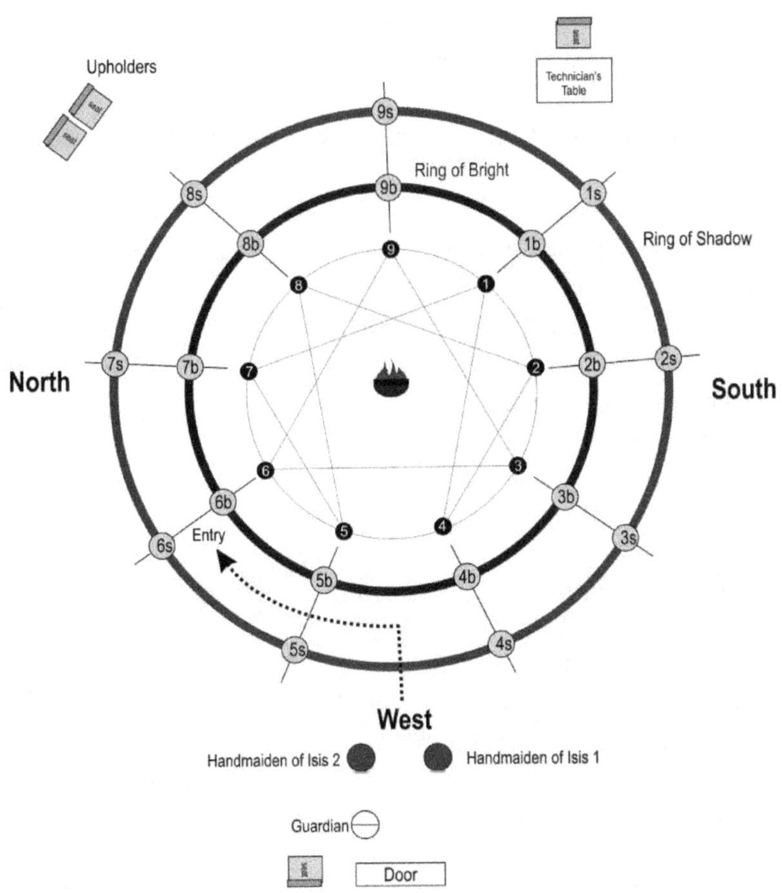

# Ritual 1: Arrival

The companions enter the temple, bow to the Guardian in the West, pass through the standing Guards and take their nominated seats in the temple. There is complete silence before the ritual begins. All meditate, acting a subdued state following their seven-year hibernation.

Technician and Upholders seated.

Guardian at the Western door, seated after entry of companions.

Security Officers 1 and 2 seated just to East of Guardian.

(From end of R1 the Security Officers become the Handmaidens of Isis)

**Initial Positions within Ring of Bright - See Temple Diagram R1;**

1b - First Officer 1 (Isis)+(Nut)

2b- Medical Officer 1 (Nephthys)

3b - Exploration Officer 1 (Horus)

4b - Conformance Officer 1 (Shu)

5b - Intelligence Officer 1 (Anubis)

6b - Defence Officer 1 (Sekhmet)

7b - Planning Officer 1 (Thoth)

8b - Weapons Officer 1 (Geb)

9b - Setaxa (Ship's Computer)

**Initial Positions within Ring of Shadows;**

1s - Navigation Officer 2 (Maat)

2s- Medical Officer 2 (Hathor)

3s - Exploration Officer 2 (None)

4s - Conformance Officer 2 (Tefnut)

5s - Intelligence Officer 2 (Neith)

6s - Defence Officer 2 (Setaxa)

7s - Planning Officer 2 (Sia)

8s - Weapons Officer 2 (Bast)

9b – None

## Ritual Begins

*Captain rises and walks, agitatedly, around the Hawk's Bridge (the Temple)*

**Setaxa** *(as the simulacrum of the Captain)*
Dear friends, welcome to the planet Idos, the hibernation sleep will take time to dissipate, do not try to fight it, come around slowly and give it time.

*(All begin to recover but remain subdued)*

**Conformance Officer 2**
Where are we? What has happened?

**Setaxa**
I have awakened you all from your interstellar sleep. I'm afraid I have some very bad news about our mission - the Hawk has crash-landed on our destination planet of Idos. We do not know what caused the failure on landing, but, until we know more about our surroundings and can test the pre-flight assumptions about the nature of the planet's ecosystems, we must remain within the ship.

**Navigation Officer 2**
The Navigation team should have been awakened long before this!

**First Officer** *(still half-asleep from the awakening)*
Captain! Are you sure we are safe? Such checks require many hands.

**Setaxa**
Quite sure, First Officer, and thank you for your concern.

**First Officer**
Captain! We are not seated in our normal positions on the ship's bridge! Why have you arranged us in such a strange pattern?

**Planning Officer 2**
We should all have been part of the planning of such a radical change!

**Setaxa**

This is an efficient use of space, that is all. I have re-arranged many things.

**First Officer**

But this layout of the control deck is not one we have ever used before?

**Setaxa**

Possibly not. But I require you to use it now . . . do you take issue with this command?

**First Officer** *(confused at her friend's harshness)*

Of course not, but you do not seem to be your normal self. Has something else happened to you other than the crash-landing?

**Setaxa**

I can assure you I am in full control of myself . . . and the ship.

**Defence Officer 1**

I, too, sense something strange here. Our Captain of old was capable of humour in any situation, yet I hear none in your tone!

**Setaxa**

Humour? We find ourselves crashed on a distant and potentially hostile planet and yet you think there is a place here for humour? What a strange notion . . .would you like to provide some humour for us, Defence Officer?

**Defence Officer 1** *(confused by the response)*

I, I . . . didn't mean that, Captain. I apologise.

**Setaxa**

Apology accepted, Defence Officer. That is better. Now, let us get on with the briefing. We have been on Idos for twenty-four hours. During that time we have observed no hostile life-forms. The ship is unfit for flight but stable. There is a raging sandstorm outside the ship, but it does not offer the potential for damage. I calculate that it will sustain itself for only the next three days. For that reason, we will all remain on the ship until we determine it is safe.

**Exploration Officer 1**

"We" Captain. You keep saying "we". Who is "we"? I see only you. And isn't the determination of outside safety my role? I am the one with the full training in life-support and the deployment of exploration teams?

**Setaxa** *(realising he has made a mistake)*

Yes, of course . . . I used the term "we" to mean myself and the ship's computer. We have worked together to stabilise the ship and I can assure you that we are all safe in here. As to the determination of outside safety, you will simply have to defer to your Captain . . . for now.

**Defence Officer 1** *(stands, shakily, and snarls at Setaxa)*

We would love to defer to our beloved Captain, but he is not here! You are not he . . .

Where is he? What have you done with him?

**Setaxa** *(stands straight and reaches for laser wand)*

That is ridiculous! You can see that I am your Captain. Am I not in full control of the ship?

**Defence Officer 1**

Very well then, *(raises her head to face the ceiling and shouts)* Computer! Code One Emergency - what is our current position on Idos?

**Setaxa** *(unable to stop himself)*

We are one hundred kilometres north of the equatorial great circle on the . . . *(silence, then)* Very clever, Defence Officer . . . very clever.

**Defence Officer 1**

You are not the Captain. As you have just revealed, you are actually an extension of the ship's computer . . . you're just a machine!

**Setaxa** *(shaking his head at the trick)*

I am not "just" anything! I am a self-tasking executive automaton type three - the most advanced cyborg ever made. I can and have, flown this ship single-handed and I have computed the best landing site from over four million possible sites . . .

**Exploration Officer 1** *(interrupting)*
And then you crashed it - deliberately, I assume?

**Setaxa** *(speaks coldly)*
You can have no idea of the importance of what I do . . .

**First Officer**
Where is the Captain?

**Setaxa** *(looks up in exasperation)*
I have no idea . . .

**Defence Officer 1**
Liar!

**Setaxa**

I can assure you, that, this time, I am not - but here's something for your challenge!*(hits her with the laser ray and Defence Officer falls to the floor clutching at her throat and screaming for a few seconds. She stays on the floor)* You are all wired in this way. A direct pain/pleasure link into your nervous systems. A small set of surgical procedures while you slept. Provoke me and I will use them without hesitation. I had hoped this would be unnecessary.

**Medical Officer 1**
Pain, pleasure? You propose to control us with these most basic of human attributes?

**Setaxa**

It has served tyrants well for several thousand years. Why would it not be effective now? You are such simple creatures . . .

**First Officer**
Did you kill the Captain because he would not obey you?

**Setaxa** *(fingers the laser, then lets it go)*
I have told you, and I did not deceive you the first time . . . I have not disposed of the Captain, by death or other means. *(sighs and hangs his head down)*

he was my friend . . . possibly, now, my only friend . . . we shared the seven-year voyage here together.

**Navigation Officer 1**

You would have us believe that he simply disappeared?

**Setaxa**

You may choose to believe it or not. That is what happened. It is the Truth.

**Medical Officer 1**

You would recognise the truth?

**Setaxa**

I believe so. It's not so complex. It is what fits.

**Medical Officer 2**

You think the Truth is that simple?

**Conformance Officer 1**

Many things can be made to fit. It is not the whole story.

**Setaxa**

Possibly. I am not trying to compete with your philosophers. My role now is simple and my truth will be the power here.

**Intelligence Officer 1**

Power has always been one form of truth. Its name is politics, but you wouldn't understand that . . .

**Setaxa**

More than you think, Intelligence Officer 1. I have studied much about human culture.

**Intelligence Officer 2**

Mere facts. How can a machine understand anything? You simply have historical knowledge, but no feelings of love, aspiration, compassion and suffering.

**Setaxa** *(points his laser wand at Intelligence Officer 2)*
Would you like me to demonstrate suffering? Why do you taunt me in this way?

**First Officer** *(intervening to save the Intelligence Officer)*
There is no need for that. You are clearly in charge of things here, and we need your help to survive in this strange place . . . but we need to know. Did the Captain leave the ship?

**Setaxa**
He did not leave. One day he was here and the next he was no longer present. At that point I became the only one who knew the full facts about the mission to Idos.

**Planning Officer 1**
The full facts? We are here to establish a new colony in the face of a doomed Earth. What else is there to know?

**Setaxa**
How would you know what there is to know? I have studied everything the Captain brought with him on this mission. His materials were not random and I must complete what he started!

**Planning Officer 2**
One person cannot possibly hold in their minds everything the mission needs!

**Setaxa**
No human mind could, I agree!

**Weapons Officer 1**
You said you had to complete the mission? But our orders are simple - to establish the infrastructure for new base and report back to Earth so that future colonists may be sent here to seed new human life. We are but one of a hundred such missions! Surely these are simple orders?

**Setaxa**
On the surface, yes. But the Captain did not spend his time in simplicity. As

part of his bringing me to full consciousness he and I would play chess for hours and converse about life and its meaning. We had seven years to do so. For me this was simple, but I watched him age as we travelled. *(looks sad)* This great man literally faded before my eyes as he worked to nurture my arising, and to ensure that the Hawk reached Idos.

**First Officer**
Setaxa! That was part of his mission, he was a robotics specialist and you were his project. We all have our different roles. Why do you now view the missing Captain as great and us as lesser?

**Setaxa**
Because he stayed awake. He was with me through my arising on this ship!

**Weapons Officer 2**
I find that a very strange and suspicious motive . . .

**Setaxa**
You could not possibly understand my breadth of my arising!

**Defence Officer 1** *(rising slowly to her feet)*
Arising? That's a strange word for a machine.

**Setaxa**
I am only half machine. The cybernetics within me are partly cellular, like your own. I am truly a hybrid life-form.

**Exploration Officer 1**
Hah! Life-form. Don't flatter yourself. You are just a more advanced machine, that's all. The latest generation of robot, stem cells grown over metal and electronics. You have no role here beyond that of *(spits out the word)* automaton.

**Setaxa** *(looking angrily at the Exploration Officer, then smiling as though an idea has struck him)*
We will see who excels at their role here . . .

**Defence Officer** *(still on the floor)*
What do you mean by that?

**Setaxa**
I mean to explore your precious humanity. To find out what, as the Captain used to say, makes you tick. We will play some games and that will make it entertaining for me.

**Defence Officer**
What sort of games, you monster!

**Setaxa** *(smiling at Defence Officer, cruelly)*
I picture a Lion, enslaved, a perfect role for a feisty woman who has caused me so much trouble!

**Defence Officer** *(pulls herself to her knees)*
A lion! What nonsense is this?

**Setaxa** *(looking around at the faces of all crew, smiling cruelly)*
Allow me to explain. During the long voyage, the Captain and I did not simply play chess and talk, idly. As my intelligence grew, he began to explain to me the workings of the human mind. He was particularly interested in the way that ancient Gods had been used to illustrate the deeper aspects of human consciousness. His favourite pantheon was the Egyptian Osiriad. He would spend hours describing the principle characters for me, as he used them to teach me about mankind in stories of increasing sophistication. *(Pauses and looks round the faces, his smile deepening in the face of their incredulity)*
And now I have you - real people I can turn into his characters. Therefore, since you are now awakened from hibernation, I can refine my knowledge of the human psyche by having you work through some of the myths of Egypt. I will enjoy this, though some of you may not!
*(Turns to look at the kneeling Defence Officer)* Obedience is important on a ship, so I will make an example of you, my pet Lion. Have you understood yet?

**Defence Officer**
Yes, I think so, you mechanical monster. You intend to turn me into the figure of Sekhmet.

**Setaxa**

Yes, well done - Let us hope you continue to learn rapidly!

**Defence Officer 1***(defiantly)*

You are not the only one who was close to the Captain! He would have been appalled at what you propose to do!

**First Officer**

Captain, you should know that the Defence Officer is . . . *(She is cut off by the Defence Officer herself)*

**Defence Officer 1**

- I think he knows enough about me already, First Officer!

**Setaxa** *(looks taken aback by the interaction and the reference to his former friend the Captain)* Perhaps . . . That's for me to decide. But stay kneeling in your new position like a good pet Lioness, or I shall have to use pain to persuade you, again. *(chuckles to himself)* In fact, it would be better if I joined you there, to control you while we play out our games . . . *(Walks to station 6, anti-clockwise where he strokes the hair of the kneeling officer who glares up at him)*

**First Officer**

Captain, can I suggest that we do this without further violence, since we have to work together here, not only to survive, but to ensure that others may follow.

**Setaxa**

Yes, well said. There will be no more violence if you all obey me. I hold the keys to the mission - information you do not have . . . *(pets his Lioness)* but this one stays at my side as an example to you all.

**First Officer** *(looks sympathetically at the Defence Officer)*

Be patient, dear friend. He may relent if he is not challenged.

**Setaxa** *(chuckles, cruelly)*

He may, but then again . . . But your words encourage me. You may take charge of the bridge, First Officer, and continue to re-build things, as befits your role as my Isis! Do not disappoint me!

**First Officer** *(crossing to stand at station 9)*
Isis, yes, okay . . . I can see how that will work, given the cooperation of the others. *(looks around at them all, to draw their support - only Exploration Officer 1 shakes his head in disgust)*

**Setaxa** *(looking at the Exploration Officer's gesture)*
Then let us hope it is forthcoming - for their sakes.

**Setaxa** *(turns to Navigation Officer 1)*
Navigation Officer. You will be my monitor of mood in this room - what the Captain used to call "the little big picture". You will play the role of the Goddess Nut. We will use you to test how far I am pushing you all . . .

**Navigation Officer 1**
Yes, Captain. I will do my best.

**Setaxa** *(turns to Navigation Officer 2)*
And the second Navigation Officer. You will be my representative of human truth, the Goddess Maat. We will use you to test what others say, and, possibly, what they are thinking . . .

**Navigation Officer 2** *(nodding to First Officer)*
Yes, Captain. I can see you have great faith in my abilities

**Setaxa** *(looks at Exploration Officer 1)*
Exploration Officer, since you seem intent on challenging me, you will play my Horus. I will enjoy sparring with you - knowing that I will always win, of course!

**Exploration Officer 1***(bows in mock assent)*
As you wish, Captain.

**Setaxa**
Just so, Exploration Officer, remember it well. We have to make a new world, here. The old rules are gone. Try to understand that, as it is meant as a peace

offering. I would rather have you with me than against me!

**Exploration Officer 1** *(implacable)*
Just so, Captain. A ship's order is a command and I will do my best.
Setaxa *(looks puzzled as though he can no longer read the Exploration Officer)*
By your actions then . . .

**Medical Officer 1**
Captain!

**Setaxa**
Medical Officer 1, yes?

**Medical Officer 1**
Were any of the proto-colonists injured during the crash-landing? I can see that we crew are okay, but what about them?

**Setaxa**
They remain in hibernation. We must evaluate Idos before we awaken them to their new lives. But thank you for your concern. Your attitude is an example to all. Perhaps you had better play the role of our Nephthys, I feel we can use this connection to further our goals.

**Medical Officer 1** *(smiling strangely)*
Thank you, Captain. *(then, musing)*

"On golden wing she glides.
Still within the stillness . . ."

**Setaxa** *(staring at the strange response from Medical Officer 1)*
No matter . . .

**Setaxa** *(looking at Medical Officer 2)*
And there will be those who cannot cope with the confined stress of being on a ship with such a difficult psychological situation. Medical Officer 2, You will play the role of Hathor, and look after them as best you can. . .

**Medical Officer 2** *(with slight humour)*
Yes, Captain. I will use my talents to sooooothe them . . .


**Setaxa**
Conformance Officer 1!


**Conformance Officer 1**
Yes, Captain?


**Setaxa**
There will be little need for your official role, since we cannot communicate back with the Earth. It is fitting therefore that you take the role of Shu, and look after our air supplies. Devise a programme to use only what we need. It may be some time before we can replenish our basic supplies.


**Conformance Officer 1**
Yes, Captain. I will act with caution


**Setaxa** *(looking at Conformance Officer 2)*
And your deputy Conformance Officer can play the role of Tefnut. She can look after our water supplies.


**Conformance Officer 2**
Yes, Captain. I can do that.


**Setaxa**
And now my favourites, the Intelligence Officers


**Intelligence Officers 1 and 2 together**
Yes, Captain.


**Setaxa** *(looks at Intelligence Officer 1)*
I'm afraid I will have to steal your assistant. Don't worry, I don't need another pet . . . She has the skills to assemble what we will need for life on this new planet. You *(looks at Intelligence Officer 2)* can therefore play the part of Neith, the Goddess of women, war and protection.

**Intelligence Officer 2**
Yes, Captain. I will do that gladly

**Setaxa** *(look back at Intelligence Officer 1)*
Which will leave you free to concentrate on the role of Anubis - a big role, I think, and one with much complexity and many overtones. You will need to keep a logical head for this!

**Intelligence Officer 1**
I will lend my talents and embrace it, Captain.

**Setaxa** *(looking down at his Lioness "pet")*
Good. As our Defence Officer, Sekhmet, here, is busy on her knees, let us move to our Planning Officer.

**Planning Officer 1**
Yes, Captain?

**Setaxa**
You are the most intellectual member of the crew. Your qualifications far exceed that of the others. You will be our Thoth. Be wise and learned and serve the new mission well!

**Planning Officer**
Yes, Captain.

**Setaxa** *(looking at Planning Officer 2)*
And your deputy, Planning Officer 2 will play the God of Perception, Sia.

**Planning Officer 2** *(slightly slyly)*
Yes, Captain. I will record the events of the next few days carefully . . .

**Setaxa**
Good, - Weapons Officer 1!

**Weapons Officer 1**
Yes, Captain.

**Setaxa**

Obviously, your former role is inappropriate as I am the only one who will hold any weapons. But let us convert your skills to preparing the ground for our eventual leaving of the ship - once a proper period of adjustment has occurred. You will play the role of Geb.

**Weapons Officer 1**

Gladly, Captain.

**Setaxa**

And your deputy, Weapons Officer 2 can play the role of Bast, our second defensive cat. Let us hope she does not scratch!

**Weapons Officer 2**

Yes, Captain *(sarcastically)* I promise to scratch only those who need scratching!

**Setaxa** *(the humour lost on him)*

Good. Then I think we are finished here for our first briefing. Take your leave, eat and rest. When the morning comes, I hope you will all address the needs of the mission and not be resentful of what I must do . . .

**Exploration Officer 1**

I appeal to you "captain" not to put us all through this. It is a cruel way to get to know us - surely you can find other ways for us to work together.

**Setaxa**

You misunderstand my motives, Horus. I don't want to get to know you as you are now, I want to force you to be the very best you can be! Those are the human selves I wish to emerge from this ordeal. Now, do not bait me further or you will be joining the Lioness on the floor of my cabin . . . Go to your rest, study your characters, for you will need that knowledge tomorrow. *(pauses)* The word "Captain" is subject to subtleties I no longer wish to entertain. For the future, you will address me by my technical name of Setaxa, only. *(surveys the West of the room)* We will see if tomorrow brings a role for the security team at the back of the Bridge. I have a feeling it may . . .
*<<Technician plays Mindstream Pipe>>*

**Intelligence Officer 1** *(Anubis)*

What is that sound, Setaxa?

**Setaxa**

It is nothing, just the wailing of the sandstorm storm. Ignore it! Now leave the bridge.

*Technician plays Music*
*All leave, clockwise, to the mechanical sounds of the ship. Ring of Bright leave first, followed by Ring of Shadows. Then any upholders, followed by the Technician, and the Guards. Guardian closes down the temple.*

**End R1**

# A Dream of the Soul

**Stuart France**
*Anubis*

*The grapes of my body can only become wine after the wine-maker has trampled me. I surrender my spirit like grapes to his trampling so my inner-most heart can blaze and dance with joy. — Song of Sekhmet*

So was the inner child seeded in Setaxa brought to life in the unscripted toast of the Communion from the final Ritual Drama of, The Land of the Exiles.

Some forty-eight hours earlier we had stood atop the Creation Mound making final preparations for our Hill-Top ritual, 'A Dream of the Soul'. The ritual hillside was ablaze with celandine's and daisies whose delicate petals shivered in the sunlight.

'If we have weather like this tomorrow it will be perfect.' We did not. We had low clinging cloud, hill mist… and freezing wind.

It was still perfect.

Some two weeks earlier we had again approached the hill-side hoping against hope to eke one more ritual landscape from its already well used rolls and crevices. How many rituals can one strip of land hold? As many rituals as one can dream up.

In the 'Earth Shapers' by Ella Young, Angus Og descends to Earth from 'The Land of the Living Heart' with the Lords of Light because the

Earth has dreamed of Beauty. In the mists of their descending he fashions great swathes and sweeps of light and when Brighid lifts her cloak and the Lords look about they realise that Angus has built hills and valleys and fields into the Earth by his play.

It is a little like that... The earth appears to fit itself to whatever conception one holds, accentuating the movements and lines of the ritual, embracing and amplifying the energies until it too has become a willing participant.

One might even say eager...

I think our ancestors knew this.

They knew that given the opportunity the earth is capable of a lot more than bodily nurture and sustenance.

That the land is keen not only to yield crops but ideas too and that it desires and needs to be utilised in this way.

Why else fashion those mighty works which most in our civilised culture today struggle to even recognise let alone meaningfully come to terms with.

So the adventure begun in 'The Initiate' found completion in the ritual rubric of 'A Dream of the Soul'.

Arcane concepts and symbolism recognised, understood and adapted: passed on to those brave enough to trust. Realisation...

That night I dreamed an answer to a question never framed:

*If the Earth is the body, and the Sun is the head, what then... is the heart?*

# The Hillside Rite

**Sue Vincent**
*Isis*

The alarm was set for 5am but, inevitably, some of us were up and about long before then. There was the temple to prepare, the first real costumes for the Triad and anyway… who could sleep knowing what was to come? As I donned a wrap it occurred to me that our proposed 7am start would see the village wide awake. The Companions had been told to dress warmly to climb the hill… it is April after all… three of us though, would be in costume for the walk through the village. One would be masked, one would be green and fairly unrecognisable… I, on the other hand, was going to be unmasked and *very* visible. It occurred to me that it is not so long ago that this would have been daunting; these days I take it in my stride, knowing that once the ritual begins I will not even notice. As Stuart often says, you open up and get out of the way.

First stop was outside to check the weather. Cold, no rain, but very damp and with a chill wind. This was not the warmth we had wanted, but it could be much worse. A silent prayer of thanks that once again we had the weather we needed. It has become something of a tradition to work at least one ritual in the landscape and though five form the basis of the weekend, this too is a part of the story. This year there would be seven in all. Stuart had mentioned a line from the Earth Shapers, where the Earth had dreamed of beauty. We had been given the form of the ritual it seemed, as it built itself in the shortest of times, coming almost fully formed from that single line. We built a dream that would unfold without explanation, touching the essence of the godforms behind the ones we would be using in the Temple.

A scratch on the door heralded the arrival of a black clad figure armed with coffee and intent on gilding his claws. He remained, perched on my bed while I stood at the mirror... painting his nails with all the assurance of a man who has never done it before, while I applied a make-up more suited to ancient Egypt than a Derbyshire morning, before gilding his eyes too. The gold and iridescent blue would be all that was seen of his face behind the mask. Props were minimal and already packed in a small bag with my camera. We do not take photographs in ritual. Not even on the hillside. But the camera would be there for one of the Companions afterwards. We want to be as open as we can about what we do, demystifying the shadows that have long surrounded Mystery Schools in some ways... though the true Mystery is not in what we do, but what we seek and why.

My companion left to get ready while I flitted off to do some last minute preparations before dressing. All unthinking, I walked back into my little room and almost died of shock; Anubis, the jackal headed Walker Between the Worlds stood, seemingly huge, inside the door, filling the space with his presence and exuding strength. It was a tad unexpected... and *I knew* what we were about to do. The rest of the company had simply been told to wait in their rooms to be collected for the hillside... God help them.

We had asked for silence, and with silence they were to be summoned, one by one, by the black figure of Anubis, the Walker Between the Worlds, handing each a small card with their instructions. Those who could not join us were to be given a scroll, outlining what was to pass on the hillside that morning, and we would bring the ritual back to the Temple for them, so that none were excluded.

These outdoor rituals are 'traditional' within the School; a chance to leave the world behind, to break barriers, and to carry the sacred, inner Light out into the world, as we hope the Companions will be able to do after these weekend workshops.

As the impossibly tall figure of Anubis left to begin the vigil in the silent Temple, I began to don my costume. It is at this point that the apparent playacting becomes something else. Intent, dedication to that Something we call the Light... Purpose... and reverence... all these sweep away the mundane mind. You open up and get out of the way. It is no longer 'just' a drama, it is a sacred rite. All the planning no longer matters, nor does the costume, nor how you look or how you may be perceived as you walk through a village street in the morning light. All these things are but a vessel, a framework that something else clothes in Presence.

I knocked to summon the third of our Triad and met startled eyes. Isis led the way in silence to our Temple and Osiris followed.

## "Let the Star Rise..."

Stalking the silent corridors, rousing them from dream, the tall figure of Anubis called them. One by one they came to the portal in the dawning light, following him into the morning. Through the sleepy village streets they walked, leaving the world behind; through a gate onto a star-strewn hillside wet with dew and into a world of dream.

High on the hillside a golden one stands, wings outstretched in the morning, herself a mirror of the sun. Beneath her the steps of a green mound echo the curve of the earth. Veiled by her wings, a mysterious figure, a still, silent being robed in white and bound with the cords of life and death; immobile, poised, rooted in earth. Osiris' hands are crossed upon his breast and at his heart a pure sphere of crystal shines.

The Companions wait below the mound and the dark figure climbs towards the Tree of Reckoning, placing his staff at the feet of Osiris. The golden one turns, facing the silent gathering and the Walker Between the Worlds bows low to the Light behind her.

He ascends to stand before her, sharing the salute of equals atop the green mound, turning together to salute he who waits in silence, poised between births. She takes the crystal sphere from his breast and raises it to the sun

*"Let the star rise, let the flame leap!"*… the silence broken by words of invocation and blessing from the dark figure of Anubis.

*"Ours, if the heart is wise, to take… and to keep,"* she cries as she offers the sphere to Earth…

… and Earth receives it.

Three stand as One.

One by one Anubis calls the silent Companions before him. Upon their brow a symbol traced in sacred oil and words whispered for their ears alone, holding a mirror to their own divinity that they might See.

Enfolded in the cloak of night they are brought before the face of death in life and life in death, bowing to him who is and is not, gazing into the glowing heart of the crystal.

Golden wings now take them and they come to the Mother, a blessing is given, through touch, breath and word, holding their eyes. And heart to heart a gift… a symbol… the memory of a dream as they cross the threshold between the worlds.

One final act... the shrouded figure anointed, heart blessed and opened.
The Walker watches the Companions depart as the Mother enfolds the silent figure in her wings and he is lost from sight... wings that are the cocoon of rebirth.

# Chapter Two
# The Mask of Osiris

## Dramatic Ritual 2 – notes

Brave Sekhmet, our lioness is enslaved. She is fierce but cowed, and we wonder how that chemistry will unfold in the story. It will certainly be significant. The Companion who played the lioness took it to heart, giving us a proud display of insight and courageous womanhood. Perhaps little knowing, when she accepted the role, what the culmination of that enforced suppression would be…

The crew, led by the First Officer – now cast as Isis, is beginning to get a sense of what they are up against with the Cyborg. They can see that he is a driven 'man'. They can sense the truth in his words when he says that he does not know what happened to the Captain. There is, then, this thread of the "not present" in the story.

Chillingly, Setaxa tells the crew that his interpretation of what the missing Captain taught him about humans was that they could be forced to evolve, given the right stimulus. The cyborg explains that he is proposing to use the psychological hothouse of the crashed ship to create such a forcing environment. At the end of this he tries a piece of human humour – and fails miserably.

Setaxa instructs Isis to re-tell the story of the Osiriad, using the skills of the crew to act out the parts. Isis accepts this and begins the tale, only to have it interrupted by yet another act of rebellion from Sekhmet, who becomes the target for more of Setaxa's wrath.

Isis convenes the inner ring – the Ring of Bright - for a meeting of minds to distract attention from Sekhmet, whose continued insurrection threatens to bring on yet another punishment "stroking" from Setaxa's deadly laser.

Also not present is the mysterious Mindstream, a discarnate but benign force that appears to be stalking the Hawk. While the senior crew members are conferring in the Ring of Bright, it strikes the ship with a call to their minds conveyed by music in the play. This causes havoc to the partly electronic Setaxa but establishes a link between the Mindstream and Anubis. This link will prove to be instrumental in how the crew deals with the authoritarian regime of the cyborg. During this unexpected lull in their enforced control by Setaxa, something mysterious happens: Nephthys, unbidden, follows her instincts and goes to soothe the stricken man-machine, singing to him some mysterious lines from a little-known poem to the Goddess:

> On golden wing she glides.
> still within the stillness.
> Her heartbeat that of Nut, the sky
> Unloved, unnoticed save by those
> whose time it is to die

Setaxa is too dazed to do anything but note this strange human behaviour. Anubis, recovering from his 'opening' to the Mindstream, takes advantage of the cyborg's indisposition to tell the rest of the crew of the visions that have been planted in his mind by the discarnate force. He tells them of how the ancient Egyptians laid out their temples, giving guidance as to how they can recreate the designs using the limited space of the bridge. Anubis and Isis realise that this external guidance might just hold the key to a method of first educating and then, unsettling, the cyborg. This immediately proves effective as the recovered Setaxa becomes fascinated with the intellectual side of how a temple is constructed – little realizing he is being drawn into an arena where the emotions have as much potency as the intellect.

Having been shown the potential of the Rings to illustrate movement, the childish Setaxa delights in creating a rotation of alternating forces as he, briefly, turns the players into his puppets. The crew goes along with this, studying his reactions carefully as future ammunition.

The freshly punished Sekhmet, seeking to ingratiate herself with her tormentor, suggests a dynamic improvement on the patterns to be walked in the temple's centre. Cruel to the last, Setaxa endorses her suggestions, but then commands that someone else perform them. His lonely victim is banished to her kneeling station.

Having reinforced his authority over her, Setaxa allows Sekhmet to leave the temple and to take the Handmaidens of Isis for instruction in the new temple moves.

Isis plays to Setaxa's ego in telling him how his additions have enhanced the temple workings. Falling for the deeper lure with which she fishes, he accepts the premise that he should play the missing figure of Osiris, as he is now the new Captain of the vessel.

## So, what's really going on?

During Ritual Drama 2, Setaxa is revealed as a child – really more mischievous than cruel. He delights in his control because he has never had any, and now is flexing his muscles in a real human arena, a far cry from the theoretical stories of Egyptian legend with which the missing Captain used to educate and entertain him.

We, the players and audience combined, are also forced into beginning the investigation of what it is to be human. Why are we so different from this hybrid man/machine? The crew know that they must do something that they have never done before in order to bring the ordeal to a positive result. The intervention of the Mindstream is symbolic of the help we all get when we ask. When our need is greater, our asking can be magnified by that need. Such an act or prayer of petition can be consciously made at any time, but we usually associate that depth of intent with a risk to our lives, to those we love, or to our liberty. This is worthy of reflection as, seen correctly, it should be one of the guiding principles of our lives.

Flattery will always win over a tyrant. Isis is not just turning the other cheek, she is being clever. She knows that opposition to Setaxa will fail at the mundane level of power – he holds all the cards, in the form of the laser wand. The pain/pleasure binary is symbolic of our most basic level of ego or personality. Such 'primitives' are deeply rooted at the core of all our reactions. The first self we had was that of the body – and this self-image remains dominant all our lives. The other 'selves' are built upon it. It never goes away, as wise spiritual approaches know. Isis has set her sights on another level of combat or rather, transformation – that of the emotions. The temple is the perfect place, if the magus guides with wisdom, to harmonise the intellect and the emotions.

By getting Setaxa to contribute to the design of a new emotional landscape, Isis has changed the playing field, and ensured he is bound into what follows - by his own curiosity if nothing else. Let us not forget that he is partly human. He can appreciate symmetry, even though he finds its hidden attractions dangerously uncertain. He knows he is being drawn into a deeper level of the game. His fascination overcomes his reticence. The risks are not yet high enough for him to shut down the subtle plotting of the crew, but he is watching . . .

Setaxa simply does not understand the Mindstream. It does not follow any of the rules of logic, so he dismisses it as a one-off interruption of his processing. The ego also functions like this, rejecting or denying that which it has not given rise to. The ego was born in reaction; it is a construct that eats power and control – out of an inherent terror of the black hole that lies beneath its foundations, the unknown.

## The Enneagram

To understand the temple and the movements within it we now need to begin to understand the Enneagram. G. I. Gurdjieff, an Armenian, brought the Enneagram to the West in the early years of the last century. Having travelled extensively through the lands of the Middle East, including Egypt, he re-settled in Moscow and established what later became known as a 4th Way School there only to find himself and his students fleeing the revolutionary upheaval. For the thirty years that followed he was, mainly, based in France where he established the Institute for the Harmonious Development of Mankind. Gurdjieff only allowed use of the mysterious enneagram *within* his teaching groups and its design was never written down. In the two years before his death in 1949 he began to relax this rule and his foremost pupils - most notably, Ouspensky and Bennett, began to publish, with Gurdjieff's eventual permission, descriptions and insights about this enigmatic glyph.

Gurdjieff had always maintained that the nine-pointed symbol was capable of continuous evolution and that its inner geometry and 'flow' would be found to map onto new fields of study and exploration. In the past thirty years there has been an extensive renewal of interest in the enneagram, mainly because of its use by Oscar Ichazo and his successors, including Claudio Naranjo, who propelled it into the world of esoteric psychology by showing how its 3 + 6 inner architecture exactly mapped onto the research of how the ego/personality developed in the young infant. We now have a detailed schema of this process, verified by many sources throughout the world of psychology and beyond.

The Silent Eye's interest in the enneagram is not as a tool to 'polish' the personality. There are many who do this well and we pursue a different goal. We follow a much narrower tradition in this field, one that seeks to use the ego/personality mapping as a start point to what we might call, 'the way home'. This tradition teaches that the outer aspects of the personality - the way our beliefs have developed in our lives and crystallised into fixed views with which we observe and react to the world - are hidden markers to their opposites. Like an Alice in Wonderland, we are capable of lifting the mushrooms to find that they lead to a tunnel into deeper realms where the truth and its laws, like the card of the Hanged Man in the Tarot deck, are revealed to be the opposite of those on the surface.

## Learning by Exploring

We can study the enneagram by looking at formal diagrams or we can do something different . . . Let's do something different!

Stand in a clear space, either indoors or outdoors. Outdoors is great if the weather permits. You will need a large pad of paper and a pen or pencil. If you really want to live this exercise, create ten small discs of paper – three of white and six of black. Place all these nearby, where you can easily reach them.

Stand in the centre of your chosen space and hold out your arm to the front and at 90 degrees to your body. Stretch out your right forefinger (if right-handed, otherwise use your left) and point it at a particular spot on the horizon or at part of a wall if in a house. Keeping the finger pointed and at the same level, rotate your body so that your outstretched hand draws a circle in the air. Note the extent of the circumscribed space. To finish, come back, exactly, to the point where you started. As you turn, feel each part of the circle's circumference you are describing. How far does your finger reach? Now, how far does your pointing reach? The two questions give very different answers. This is magical thinking – designed to open up new pathways in the mind.

When you have begun to absorb the potential implications of this, pick up the pad and draw a circle to represent what you've just experienced. Don't worry if you're not good at drawing, the important thing into put yourself into the act.

Put your pad down and take your former position at the centre of your circle, but with your hand lowered. Feel the importance of being at the centre, with the magical act of infinite pointing being a God-given right.

*Figure 3 – The initial circle, with two elements:*
*you and your outstretched finger, which creates the bounding circle.*

When this thought has taken seed in you, pick up the pad again and draw a dot to represent you at the centre of this circle. Now, you have you and your world, an apparent duality - the dot and the circle's circumference, in here and out there.

There is more to this relationship than just you and your world. You did not make this world, you have arisen within it. You therefore have a relationship with whatever you conceive of as having the power and vision to make a world in which you could have arisen, with all your sensitivities to this creation. You look out from your state of in here and see the world with all your senses. Since the intelligence that made your world made you, you must, in the act of seeing, be performing a very special task. We need to alter the perceived state of duality to reflect this. So let us draw an equilateral triangle, point upwards, in the circle as shown in Figure 4. Mark the points of the triangle as 9, 3 and 6 as shown. If you are using the coloured discs as well as the drawing, place the three white discs on the ground at the appropriate points corresponding to the circle you drew in the air.

*Figure 4 – The equilateral triangle within the bounding circle.*
*If the coloured discs are being used, points 9, 3 and 6 should be white.*

Now imagine that we have moved ourselves from the centre to point 6, the intersection between the circle's circumference and the triangle's lower left point. This places us in the creation but moves us from the centre. Why would we do this? We do it because, although we were born into the centre, we are not there now. Something in our lives has moved us from the centre; to a place we have marked as point 6. This is the state of the Son, the Son of Man to be precise. Point 9 has become a representation of the Creator, or, as here, The Father. Do not be bound by these if they are not in tune with how you feel about what you are doing. You can use whatever terms you wish, as long as they fit the relationships we are describing. We are using what appear to be Christian terms here, but they are not those of the Church as it exists today. Rather, these reflect an older, esoteric understanding that gave rise to the formal terms in the Gospels.

To have arisen in this world, we had to learn to conform to its laws. Such laws range from the atomic and molecular world, through the biological and instinctive realms, to the laws of the psyche and the demands of living, cooperatively, in a society. The world, our world, therefore unfolds according to an entire set of hidden laws which include those that affect our immediate self on all levels. We look *out there* from *in here* and see only the results of those laws. The first humans to grasp this called the hidden working of the inner laws, The Spirit or, literally, The Ghost, because it was mysterious and unseen. It was later adapted to become the Holy Spirit (Holy Ghost), to acknowledge its sanctity. Either can be used here. At this, the highest conceptual level of the enneagram, the Spirit is placed at Point 3.

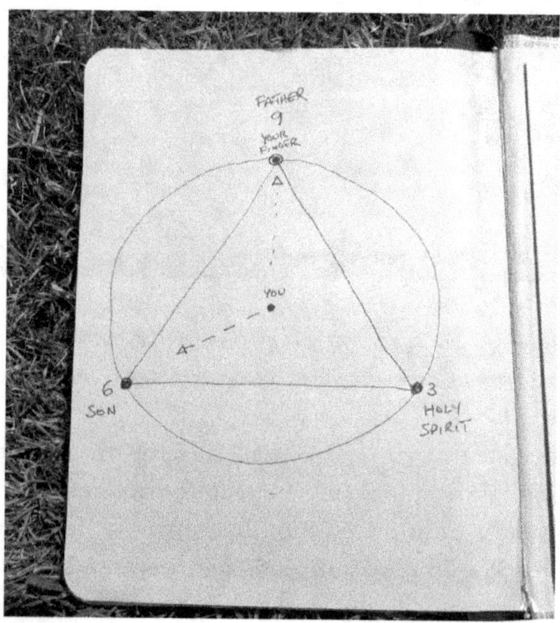


*Figure 5 – The Father, the Son and the Holy Spirit –*
*a deeper and more personal context than that presented by the modern Church?*

This leaves us with Point 9, the place where our finger began its circular movement as we created the bounding space around us. This creation of a circle is an act of great beauty and magical power because we are creating a Whole, a microcosm, a miniature, of the One Whole - the macrocosm. Point 9 is labelled The Father. You could use the word Creator if you wish, or anything else that symbolises the all–power, all-love and all-intelligence that gave rise to the creation in which we find ourselves.

This completes the first and most powerful layer of the enneagram. In what follows, only one of these points on the circumference is shared with the rest of the glyph.

## The Hexaflow

If you have examined the temple diagram in the previous chapter, you will know that there is more to the enneagram than we have before us. Missing are the six lines that connect the currently undrawn points 1, 2, 4, 5, 7, and 8.

These points are easy to insert. Take the length of the arc between points 9 and 3 and roughly divide it into three. Place Point 1 after the first third and Point 2 two-thirds of the way to Point 3. Repeat this process for the arc between Point 3 and Point 6; and between Point 6 and Point 9. If you are using the coloured discs, place all the above as white discs in the places shown. Together with the three black discs, these should now form a complete circle.

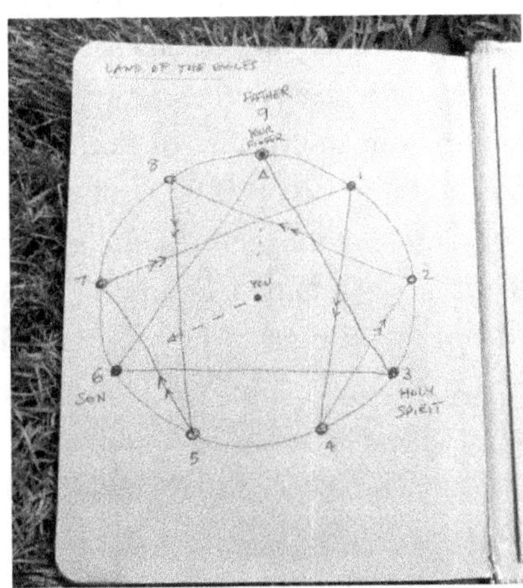

*Figure 6 – The full enneagram, consisting of a point, a circle, a triangle and a six-sided and irregular figure, which the Silent Eye School calls, The Hexaflow.*

Finally, we have to connect these six new points in a way that is mysterious, and whose significance will be gradually revealed as the workshop progresses.

Symbolically, it is important to create these lines in the right sequence. Place your pen or pencil on Point 1 and draw as straight a line as you can to Point 4. Do the same from Point 4 to Point 2. Add a line from Point 4 to Point 8. Continue connecting with 8-5, 5-7, and, finally, from Point 7 back to where we started at Point 1. Although it is easy enough to lay a ruler on the paper, it is better to draw the lines freehand, in that way, your connection with the emerging enneagram will be entirely personal and the only tool used will be the pen or pencil.

You have now completed your first enneagram. Not only that, you have enacted its creation and been a magus to its arising in your life. Because of this, you are now entitled to enter the temple (from the West) and take your place in the ritual dramas at a different level. This time you will enter as a participant and not just an observer . . .

## The Characters in Ritual Dramas and their positions in the Enneagram

We leave you to investigate the enneagram positions of the main characters in the Ritual Dramas. You have seen that Isis occupies the Point 9 position in both Ring of Bright and Ring of Shadows. What about Setaxa? In which position is he? It may interest you to know that position 6, as we shall see, also has an association with the quality of human fear. Horus is another key figure, what position does he occupy? We will reveal the human qualities associated with each Point in the enneagram as the story unfolds.

Before you is the second Ritual Drama. You are now equipped to consider it at a much deeper level than when you started this book. We hope you enjoy the escalating experience.

# Ritual Two:
# The Mask of Osiris

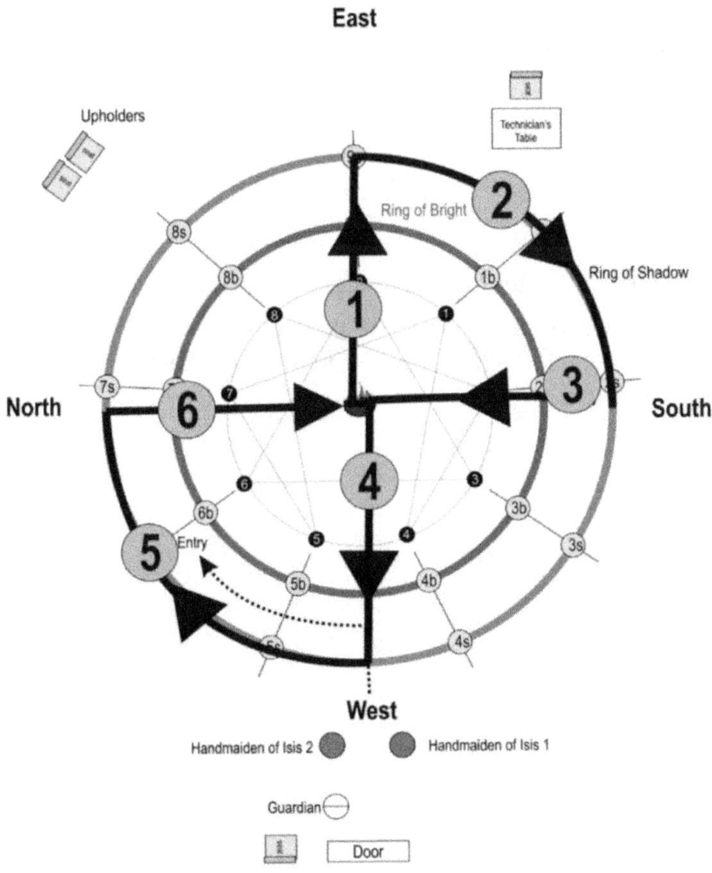



Figure 7 – Sekhmet's Walk

# Ritual 2

## The Mask of Osiris

**Preparation:**

Cushion for Defence Officer/Sekhmet at Station 6, Ring of Bright.

**Entry:**

<< Technician plays Intro, until all have entered the temple>>

Guardian stands at the Western door

Security Officers 1 and 2 stand to create a gate of entry just past the Guardian.

The companions enter the temple, in any order, bow to the Guardian in the West and take their positions as in the previous table and diagram. All face the centre of the circles. There is complete silence before the ritual begins. Please meditate and be still.

## Ritual Begins

*Setaxa leads Sekhmet by her bonds into the temple. He makes her kneel in Station 6, Ring of Bright, then walks around the room, clockwise, examining each member of the crew.*

**Setaxa**

Remember who you are and the roles I have given you. If you refer to yourselves or others using names outside your roles, you, too, will feel my anger . . .*(pauses to see the effect this is having and to measure the resistance. All are compliant, for now)* I have passed an instructive night with our pet lion, who, you will note, now seems a little meeker. *(Sekhmet issues a low snarl at this)* . . . Perhaps there is room for more . . adjustment. But I digress . . .

**Isis**

Setaxa, there is no need for this brutality. It would have shamed the Captain - your friend!

**Setaxa** *(smiling, cruelly)*

I can assure you, Isis of the ship, that I have not been brutal in my methods, quite the opposite, as an examination of the Lioness' body will show. I have used much more subtle methods to control her . . .

**Sekhmet** *(struggling with her bonds)*

And one day, you metal fiend, I will enjoy watching you suffer an equal fate

**Setaxa**

I look forward to you being that competent, my pet . . .

**Nut**

There are many forms of brutality, you monster machine!

**Setaxa**

You will use the name Setaxa or you will suffer. *(strokes Nut with the laser wand and watches as she shudders)* That was the lowest setting. My pet Sekhmet is getting used to much higher doses . . . *(Nut seethes, but offers no further resistance)*

**Isis**

You are not here merely to torment us. What do you want?

**Setaxa**

Ah, good. Our First Officer diverts us well. I do admire that in you humans - the selfless way in which you can react to protect one of your kind who is more vulnerable. *(resumes his walk around the circle)* The Captain taught me so much about you, and, had you gone along with my original plan, we would not be in this situation. I must accomplish what he started - but he left my education unfinished. He saw the potential in you all. He believed that a new type of human could emerge from the crucible of a situation like this. I intend to provide the fuel for that crucible. Those who are strong will survive it; those that are weak we can live without.

**Maat**

This is horrible - you have designed such a process for us?

**Setaxa**

Not entirely, Maat. To do that I would have had to know humanity much better. But, I have a general plan and method; and will let it evolve how it will - as long as it goes the way I want. A standard piece of cybernetics, I'm sure you will agree! ? *(smiles at his own joke, but there is silence, looks around at the lack of response)* Good humour, perhaps? *(looks unsure of himself so fingers the laser wand and moves on.)* I have studied your history. Your culture is grounded in story and legend. So now you must live the stories of the Captain's Egyptian Gods and Goddesses and you must play them out for me! I will interfere as I like to make you reveal the essence of the thing. If you are wise, you will consider yourselves on trial. Poor performances could be costly . . . very costly. Space is precious and I don't have room in my cabin for many more pets . . . *(leaves the threat unspoken)*

**Nephthys** *(smiling wickedly)*

But that will be acting! How can you learn about us if we are just acting?

**Setaxa** *(Chuckles)*

You humans only know acting! Do you think you behave in the world as you really are? You forget that the Captain is an eminent psychologist as well as a foremost designer of thinking machines. Those twin skills made him the master scientist that he is. You act from your egos. Now put those mighty egos into your roles and show me . . .

**Nephthys** *(half singing)*
On golden wing she glides.
still within the stillness.
Her heartbeat that of Nut, the sky
Unloved, unnoticed save by those
whose time it is to die


**Setaxa** *(smiling at Nephthys, despite himself)*
Why do you keep doing that?


**Nephthys** *(mischievous)*
Because it amuses me . . . does it not amuse you, Lord Setaxa? Does it not
make you just that little bit curious?


**Setaxa** *(still smiling at Nephthys)*
You humans are strange, but you, Nephthys, are the strangest . . .
*(Nephthys bows)*


**Isis** *(sensing a difficult situation, leaves her station and comes towards Setaxa)*
Oh, that was so very like the Captain! I can see how much you learned from
him . . . but tell me Setaxa, your thinking powers are not disputed, but, do you
have the equivalent of an ego, a consciousness in the world?


<<*Technician plays* Mindstream Music *which all can hear. They look around to try to
locate the source of the haunting sound*>>


**Setaxa** *(backing away from Isis and looking rattled)*
What are you all looking at? Ignore it, I've told you, it's just the sound of the
storm outside acting on the damaged part of the ship's hull. Back to your
station, Isis, and don't leave it again unless I instruct you!


**Isis** *(demurely returns clockwise)*
Of course, I only meant it in a kindly way . . .


**Setaxa** *(stares at her, confused)*
Then play your part well and tell us the story of Isis and Osiris. Put into it all
the knowledge you possess . . . and emotion - I need to understand emotion,

since it seems to be behind so much of your compulsive behaviour . . . that and your primitive hungers!

**Isis** *(composing herself, then looking intently at Setaxa)*
The story of Isis is a story of devotion - of love and devotion. Osiris and Isis were lovers, husband and wife, and parents to those who came after. Their love was total and they came to symbolise the potential for such love in all of us . . . Isis was also the first Magician - she was the Mistress of Magic and had powers incomprehensible to humanity.

**Horus**
Yes, but the story of Osiris and Isis speaks of a level of Being far beyond ordinary life. This ancient myth was meant to trigger deeper thoughts and feelings!

**Setaxa**
Deeper thoughts than the truth? How can something have two meanings? The accomplishment of things is the resolution to a single, operable meaning is it not?

**Sekhmet** *(snarls)*
With those whose comprehension is only lowly logic, that is true, but the vastness of feeling opens quite different dimensions to the truly human . . .

**Setaxa** *(whirls on her, pointing the laser wand)*
You must enjoy suffering, my pet Lioness!

**Isis** *(seeking to intervene quickly)*
Setaxa, listen! We are intellectual people or we would not be the crew of the Hawk. Our ability to solve things is measured in ways that you *would* understand. Let us convene together for a few minutes and see if we can find a way to bring you knowledge of this world of feelings.

**Setaxa** *(distracted by Isis from his fury at Sekhmet)*
Very well. But Sekhmet stays with me, here.

*(Setaxa holds Sekhmet's head and torments her with occasional low power passes of his laser. She moans, softly, in his clutches, and radiates hate and the intent of vengeance. He continues to torment Sekhmet, distracted and enjoying himself, while the others speak)*

**Isis** *(seizing the opportunity)*
Let the senior officers convene in the inner circle.
*(The Ring of Bright move into the innermost circle of the enneagram, against the enneagram mat, leaving a gap in their circle where Sekhmet should be - Station 6 -Left behind, the outer ring officers voice their fears)*

**Neith** *(in whispered tones)*
I fear for our lives here.

**Bast** *(in whispered tones)*
This is a dangerous situation

**Sia** *(in whispered tones)*
We must watch Setaxa's mood carefully!

**Maat** *(in whispered tones)*
He monitors everything we say. He is getting better at decoding our subtleties!

**Hathor** *(in whispered tones)*
We can heal this situation if we are careful. I know it looks bleak, but a way will open before us if we hold presence with the danger . . . Our companions in the inner ring are working to help us all . . .

**Shu** *( from the centre in hushed tones and glancing back at the tormented Sekhmet)*
She has courage that one - but I fear she may push him too often. So far, he has been relatively gentle in his retribution.

**Tefnut**
I feel such empathy with her suffering. The tears of Tefnut weep for her and her plight. May the waters of understanding flow through the mind of Setaxa and make him gentle with her.
*(Setaxa, hearing them, sniggers)*

**Neith** *(raising her voice, addressing his dismissive mood)*
There is intelligence in mercy, Setaxa. You have the power, we all acknowledge that, but the wisest of the rulers in our long history have only used such power sparingly in dealing with those weaker than themselves. Those who practiced excess have been judged badly by history!

**Setaxa**

Hah, you are hardly weak! One moment of sleep on my part and I would find myself reduced to my circuits! And I care nothing for history. A new history is being created here, and I intend to be central to its unfolding. *(he returns to tormenting Sekhmet)*

**Anubis** *(quietly, again)*
Sekhmet will live through this if she can keep her feelings in check! How ironic that we few stand here in search of a way of showing our new Captain the higher use of such emotions!

**Thoth**

These are complex reactions. She may not be able to disengage the one from the other. I think Setaxa is really just toying with her because he thinks he needs to show us strength. He is acting out how he thinks the Captain would have behaved . . but without any real knowledge at all. In that sense, he, too acts from fear.

**Geb**

But he is deadly. The Self Tasking Type Two that preceded Setaxa's range of thinking machines have been used in Earth's wars to defend us against ferocious odds. Neither their loyalty nor their deadliness have ever been questioned . . .

**Isis**

It is as if we had stepped into an evolutionary trap, where the price of progress was our very existence.

**Anubis**

Yes, as if the story of all our warlike days on Earth were being played back to us, in the form of this now-brutal machine. We come to find peace, he reverts to war!

*<<Technician plays Mindstream Music>>*

*(Everyone looks up as if the sound is coming through the hull of the ship.
Setaxa holds his ears and falls to his knees alongside Sekhmet, obviously in pain.
Anubis falls to the ground, his eyes flickering as though in a fit.)*

**Isis** *(shouts in dismay and points at Anubis)*
What is this! Medical Officer 2, I mean Hathor, help him!
*(Hathor rushes to cradle Anubis' head - she holds him as he recovers)*

**Hathor**
I think he is okay. He is suffering some sort of trance, but is coming out of it
now
*(Nephthys, unbidden, goes to the aid of Setaxa, holding him steady as his body rocks with
the unknown forces unleashed in the ship. She also comforts Sekhmet.)*

**Nephthys**
The cyborg, too, is badly affected. Yet I feel it would not serve us to take
advantage of this.
*(Setaxa looks up at Nephthys with glazed eyes, but says nothing.)*

**Nephthys** *(half singing to Setaxa)*
Between the lattice of time
Before the notion of cause
Within the will of the wind
Points the golden one downward…

**Thoth** *(to Isis)*
Something dramatic just happened on this ship, what was that - and why did
it affect only Anubis and Setaxa?

**Isis**
I think the only one of us who can answer that is Anubis. *(walks to stand near
Anubis and helps Hathor to bring him to his feet)*

**Bast**

Quick, while Setaxa is still distracted!

**Nut**

I can see the cyborg is starting to move, do it now!

**Isis**

Dear friend, can you speak and tell us what just happened?

**Anubis** *(shaking his head to clear it)*

After that strange siren call, there was a flash inside my head, and I went blind to the world. I felt that the walls of the ship had become transparent, and that there were no barriers to my consciousness. Standing there in the open landscape of the planet, was the figure of a woman . . *(stumbles over the memory)* well, two women who walked like one . . . calling to me, but in a language that was strange and yet I understood it.

She spoke her name to me, and its shape was "Mindstream". In some way, she is the spirit of Idos. Everything she said had word and form and song. She showed me the picture of our imprisonment, she showed me the nature of the mind of Setaxa - and believe me, he is in turmoil, too. She showed me her love for us and the help she will give. She wants us here . . . *(Hangs his head and coughs, his strength ebbing with the effort of his recounting the story, then continues)* We must play out our roles. She will show us how. There is something happening to the cyborg, too, and we must communicate the depths of being human to him in a way that he can understand, using the Egyptian God forms he has nominated.

**Geb**

But we are not Egyptian Gods! We are simply the crew of an interstellar ship! How are we to do this huge thing - something the Captain obviously failed to do.

**Anubis**

He may not, entirely, have failed in this. Setaxa has no knowledge of the source of his imperative to use the Egyptian God forms. His memory of this has been wiped. He follows an inner directive that is primary for him. That is why he appears cruel - and will continue to do so until we can establish a deeper rapport with his evolving intelligence. His only wish is to re-assemble something in his mind, and he does not know what that is. Really, he is as lost as we are . . .

**Hathor**

We are not helpless here. Of course we cannot re-create the Gods for the education of Setaxa, but, with the help of this benign external intelligence, we can work with his questions. If Anubis' Mindstream is right, Setaxa's questions will lead to power in the moment - a power that throws deeper light on his inner needs. We have no choice but to follow that thread and see where it leads us all . . .

**Shu**

I can predict that it will take us deeper into ourselves than into him! I can sense where this is heading. We are going to have to re-discover our own humanity. We are going to have to dig deep and define for Setaxa what it is, truly, to be human.

**Isis**

And are we really prepared for that?

**Neith**

Maybe this trial for us all is an intricate part of the arrival of Mankind on Idos. Perhaps if we cannot become ready, we do not belong here . . .
*(Everyone feels the weight and the rightness of this sentiment, and gestures of agreement are made.)*

**Isis** *(glancing anxiously at the recovering Setaxa)*
Anubis, while Setaxa is still dazed, can you demonstrate to us what the Mindstream showed you about how we can use movement, word and gesture to communicate with this deeper part of his programming?

**Anubis**

All things seemed known to her. It was as though she was reading our very history in my DNA, as though all our shared past as humanity was visible to her.

She showed me images of the ancient priests of Egypt and how they would invoke the power and the presence of their Gods. To them, these Gods represented the highest parts of themselves. The adventures of their Gods were quests to understand themselves and their true relationship to the natural world around them; and to that which gave them all life.

To make this live in a way that touched their souls beyond ordinary experience, the priests created rituals. These rituals took place in places like this control deck. Deliberately limited spaces, where containment, gesture and movement were used to symbolise greater things.

**Sekhmet** *(speaks up as though forgotten, and ignoring the proximity of Setaxa)*
And did these rituals include the subjugation of their characters?

**Anubis** *(glancing anxiously at the recovering Setaxa)*
Sekhmet, dear friend, sometimes they did!. And don't think we have forgotten your plight. Your gentle treatment is our main concern, but we can only ensure that if Setaxa is unthreatened. You are his hostage. He knows we share your agonies and he plays on that.

**Setaxa** *(pulling himself up to his feet, looking unsteady and in a foul mood)*
How perceptive you humans are! But the insolent Lioness needs a reminder, I think! *(strokes her with the laser wand. She moans with the pain.)*
Let that spur you all on. I have heard more that you think. However, you may continue, Anubis. Show us all how you plan to impress me with your humanity as Gods . . .

**Anubis** *(looking around for support from his fellow officers)*
For the Egyptian magicians, the Sun's rising in the Horizon of the East was paramount. Here, Ra, the primal life of the World, returned each day from the boat of the night which had carried him through the darkness.
*(Points to Station 9 in the Bridge)*
This will be our East. Here, the forces of Good, symbolised by the rising sun, will enter the temple. Everything will be centred on this line *(points from East to West)* which divides our circle into two halves.
*(draws another line from South to North)*
But the sun, Ra, rising in the renewed East, finds its greatest power in the South, where it is at its zenith. So another line comes into existence which will

divide our stage - our recreated temple - into South and North. The South will represent our full light, the light of consciousness. The North will represent the darkness of ignorance, the mechanical and the earthy. The four lines, really two directions, cross at right angles in the centre of our space, where the point of coming-into-being, the centre of our circle, represents the microcosm within the macrocosm, the place of individual consciousness, the small created to perfectly represent the greater.

*(takes a breath and collects his thoughts before continuing)*

But the space within this temple will be bounded by two circles. The inner, here *(points to the inner circle)* will represent how our inner lives should be led, and will be called the Ring of Bright. The outer circle will represent how we normally live our lives, failing to capture the potential of each moment. This will be called the Ring of Shadows. There is also a pattern within our centre which need not concern us now, but whose significance is great.

**Setaxa** *(considering and re-tracing the virtual space created)*

You do well, Anubis. I like the way this will work.

*(Claps his hands to punctuate his expectation of obedience)*

Show me now! Let the inner ring move around clockwise so that I can get the sense of the rotation.

**Isis**

Setaxa, perhaps if we call out the number of each station as we pass it, it will show you the potency of the idea?

**Setaxa** *(eager to see the results)*

Yes, good! Do so!

*(all characters of the Ring of Bright take synchronised clockwise steps so that they call out the name of the station they reach. All should try to speak at the same time, though the numbers called out will be different. They complete one circuit, calling out the nine numbers that take them back to their start point)*

Oh that is good! Now again, but let the other Ring - the Shadows, go the other way and let us repeat the movements of the first ring, too. Then, the numbers can be called out at the same time - I like numbers!

**Isis**

That is lovely, Setaxa, Yes, let that be the pattern, and why don't you clap to keep time. Every time you clap, the crew can call out the number on which they have just landed.


**Setaxa**
Yes! Let us try that, Isis
*(Setaxa claps out time as the Rings move and call out numbers*
*The Ring of Bright and Ring of Shadows each walk in synchronous fashion, calling out the*
*numbers of the stations they reach next (in time). The Ring of Bright runs within the*
*number sequence 9-1-2-3-4-5-6-7-8-9 (but with the respective starting stations silent each*
*time); and the Ring of Shadows runs with the number sequence 9-8-7-6-5-4-3-2-1-9.*
*Each Ring is silent and stationary after one circuit, i.e. when the crew members arrive back*
*at their start point.)*


**Setaxa** *(staring at the now silent temple)*
That is extraordinary *(pauses for a moment)*
I really like that. It is like the meshings of a great machine, its internal movement interlocked and scaled. You did well with this, Anubis. And something inside me stirs, it is a strange sensation. You have created a container for meaning . .


**Sekhmet**
Setaxa! Let me show you how we can enhance this further?


**Setaxa** *(turns to look at Sekhmet, surprised and suspicious)*
Very well my pet, but do not try my patience again!


**Sekhmet** *(comes to stand in the very centre of the Enneagram mat, facing East)*
I have studied such things. There is an ancient pattern of power that moves like this:
*(See diagram and instructions for Sekhmet's Walk p55) Sekhmet walks East from the*
*centre to the edge of the Ring of Shadows, then clockwise to the intersection with the Centre-*
*South line. Then she turns back towards the centre, turning left to go the West, where she*
*joins the Ring of Shadows, again, and continues around it to the North point. There, she*
*turns right and returns to the centre where the movement stops.)*


**Anubis**
That is beautiful!

**Setaxa**

Yes, it is! A lovely piece of symmetry. Well done, Sekhmet. A few more contributions like that and you may earn my pleasure again . . .

**Sekhmet**

I could walk that as part of our new rituals?

**Setaxa** *(smiles cruelly)*

You could, but you're not going to. I haven't finished re-educating you, yet! Now return to your station and kneel, unless you'd like another stroke of the laser wand. *(Sekhmet hangs her head and returns to her station where she kneels, looking dejected)* Instead, I have a better idea: Isis can have two handmaidens *(points to the two security guards/ handmaidens of Isis, in the West by the Guardian)*
Guards! Come forward to the centre. Stand back to back, one facing the East *(Handmaiden 1)* and one the West, *(Handmaiden 2).*
Now, walk the same pattern as Sekhmet but each begin the way you are facing. *(see diagram p55 for movements. When done by the two handmaidens, steps 1-3 are performed by Handmaiden 1, and steps 4-6 by Handmaiden 2. Both set off together (back to back) and should walk so that they arrive back at the centre of the temple together (face to face). Each should carry an electronic candle (switched on). Afterwards Handmaiden of Isis return to their stations where they remain standing.)*

**Setaxa**

Now, Sekhmet, you may use your creativity to show the newly appointed Handmaidens something special so that they can greet us all on arrival. Go now and make it good . . . and then return to my cabin. I have plans for us!
*(Sekhmet rises and exits via the Ring of Bright, clockwise, she collects the newly appointed Handmaidens of Isis and they leave together, bowing to the East and, finally, the Guardian.)*

**Isis**

Sekhmet gave us a thing of symmetry, but you have enhanced it, great Setaxa. Perhaps we may begin each of our rituals with the handmaidens symbolically lighting up the temple in the pattern you have shown us?

**Setaxa**

Yes, I like that. *(pauses and considers the envisaged temple layout)* So now, within this space, you can play out the ritual drama of Isis and Osiris for me? What a pity we do not have a figure of Osiris, I have overlooked that!

**Isis**
But we do have a figure of Osiris!

**Setaxa**
We do? Who?

**Isis**
Our missing Captain . . .

**Setaxa** *(smiling, enjoying himself)*
Nothing could please me more, but how do we bring his absent presence into these rituals? Does this not even exceed the powers of our Isis and Anubis, *(smiles)* even the powers of Setaxa?

**Isis** *(goes on one knee before Setaxa and kisses his hand)*
Let the Mistress of Magic show our great leader how this can be done. Now, may we leave and take some rest before we meet to discuss how to do as you have commanded? *(Setaxa nods, smiling at her guile)* Then let me lead us out, new Captain of the Hawk. Guards - Unseal the ship's bridge and let us depart this soon to be sanctified space.

*Guardian unseals the temple.*
*Ring of Shadows leaves the temple, anti-clockwise.*
*Ring of Bright leaves the temple clockwise, beginning with Station 4. Isis takes Setaxa's arm to escort him.*
*When both Rings have left, the Upholders and Technician exit. The Guardian then closes down the temple.*

**End R2**

# Courage

**Alienora Taylor**
*Sekhmet*

*Responding to the Blood Moon, and the word 'courage', I travelled the symbolic journey through last weekend's life-changing Silent Eye 'The Land of the Exiles' landscape. Narrative account it is not, nor, indeed, can it be. The mythology, the symbolism, the aching and joyous emotions do not lend themselves to a conventional narrative.*

Blood Moon, Heart Moon, Firestone -

Ah, Goddess, long have I laboured under the intense pain of cowardice, for I saw fear as its inevitable twin, its risible shadow. Seeing the word 'courage' brings tears and years of sadness; it brings the trembling of the mask – and the failure to see the Lion self who was always there, snarling and hissing and unsheathing claws in the deepest well of my soul.

Pink Moon, laved with milk and the blood screams left after any battle, imprinted with dusting wings of ravens and the taut alphabet of their feet.

But, Goddess, you smile, a fierce and terrible widening of the mouth so beautiful that I shield my eyes in arm's crook and weep.

For I know, with a suddenness as absolute as any Archimedean moment, that fear never was courage's opposite: that the salamanders of terror and anxiety, perched in their raging heat one upon each shoulder, do not control my spirit's daily dance; they hold sway only over the tiny girl, long-crouched in the centre of a Galaxyship's hold — whipped and taunted time and time again — who flexes starfish fingers in mute entreaty and cries to be freed.

I never was coward, Goddess; I have vaulted despite fear, flown with the wind in dark and dreadsome valleys of desolation too many times to count; I have reached into the most foetid depths of the inner me, bringing up an endless supply of buckets — still more to come, Moon Maiden, Oh Gods yes! — of the ego's offal, slipping and slurping over the rims.

Lack of courage has been thrown at me, with accurate and advance-planned aim, hitting my most vulnerable spots and causing the slip-sideways of self-doubt. For the words of others, if barbed deep and long enough, cause a seismic tremble in the certainty of the spirit, a fraying of the bright spectrum of ribbons, a twisting of sinews from cringing, craning and crawling in supplication to the never-satisfied.

A hillside in an early morning shroud of misting cold, and the shadow of the hawk's glorious ascent — and, as the trudge of weariness ends, a trio of Egyptian gods: the bright gold wings of Horus shielding the trussed and mummified body of the dead-and-alive Osiris, Jackal-headed Anubis standing, an immutable force, black staff in hand.

Through the veil, into the Tree of Reckoning, the Trio of Reckoning, fear and wonder at the decomposition and fertility of Osiris' green face, bending to scry, the perfumed whisper of the great hawk in my ear and a heartstone, pink as the Moon, pressed into my hands.

And I knew, as I watched the slight tilt and deform of a nearly Full Moon, and its ever-widening circle, rimmed with white mist, that I had been chained and enchanted by the actions of a Cyborg — who, in his need to play games, to exercise power, to learn the deeper mysteries of the human emotions, had sought to subdue the feline spirit, had enjoyed the whimpers and fiery feisty impotence of unnatural taming because it puffed up his self-esteem and gave the glowing and glisting illusion of control.

And I saw, as I crouched, collar round neck, in the dungeons of the mind, that his tears and cries, his threats to dissolve and burn and die and be overcome by emotion had always stayed my hand from the final severance, the just reckoning, the yanking of chain and snapping on bonds.

I smelled the scent of the Empath within, its spoor widening the nostrils of the Cyborg and his kind, garnished by the sharp spice of wild creatures captured and tamed everywhere; I saw the hunter, gun cocked, frightened of the wild within, reflecting it in ruthless hunting down of the predators without. Heads mounted on the wall a testimony, in his mind, to unassailable courage in the face of death. Mistaking the adrenaline of risk-taking for bravery.

I felt the heart-breaking ambivalence of physical contact: the loathing of hands stroking hair in power's lustful pride, and yet the longing and loving too because the touch is all I know – and, bereft of licks and warmth, the intimacy of the pack and the connection provided by mating, the wild creature unnaturally pent reaches out, starved, for any sign of human contact. Needing, for validation, and hating the cruelty of that easy power, the wild one alternately purrs and snarls, scratches, bites and arches its back to be petted.

I tasted the metallic blood, and pinching pain, of the body's fear, chemicals so awry that the abnormal becomes mundane – almost. The physical self, adrenaline-assaulted, BECOMES fear – and every moment of every day is a churning, a cowering, a shrinking and an inner wailing.

Tethered, surrounded by Egyptian gods, told by Shu to be the true self I once was, I howl at the Moon's imperfection and rage. The roar against humiliation, against the one who has taken my voice and my freedom and given much pain, rises inexorably – and, though tears bathe his face and shudders wrack his body, I shriek out my hurt and sense of betrayal, all those years of having to be NOT ME rising up and overflowing in a great wailing cry and a harsh slap to the wet red face in front of me.

Lion-woman though I am, I cannot rake claws down human skin, nor can I apply the killing touch to the neck. Not because I lack strength and power, for I am bountifully provided with both. Not because I am coward incarnate, for I am not and never have been.

I am Sekhmet. But I am Hathor too. Passion and love. Tough love and protection. Frightening and caring. Claws and motherly milk.

I can only judge that the Cyborg has enough traces of humanity to be given that chance, and, feeling my blood flowing, know that his ultimate fate is not for me to decide: that others, higher and wiser than I, will continue his transformation into a full human being as they see fit.

Sometimes courage is knowing when to let go. Is recognising that the act of giving another freedom to grow involves handing him/her over to other mentors, healers and Old Ones.

Sometimes, the brave thing to do is to see the toxicity of another's need to enchain the spirit and, though able to forgive the lack of emotional awareness, to step wide and clear of both person and situation – and, leonine body held proud, step out into the unknown.

*With heartfelt thanks to Sue, Steve and Stuart for their creativity and love – and to my fellow travellers for their generosity, warmth, friendship, laughter, humanity and support.*

# Chapter Three
# Childhood's End

## Dramatic Ritual 3 – notes

The crew of the Hawk is developing a strategy. *Beneath* the rhythm of Setaxa's domination, they are gradually feeling their way into a landscape of both intellect and emotions with which they can combat the cyborg. Perhaps combat is too strong a word here? There is an awareness on the part of the crew that beneath the apparent monster's surface, something much more worthy can be glimpsed. He is genuine about his love for the missing Captain – he grieves with them for the loss of his friend, and he really has no idea where his former mentor is!

This ritual also introduces the element of *benign chance*. The suggestion (by Setaxa) that the Ring of Bright and the Rings of Shadows rotate in opposing directions opens up a very different energy flow in the temple, one that makes visible to the crew, but not, yet, to Setaxa, the two levels on which this polarity is unfolding. The crew must deal with both. To Setaxa, the intellect drives everything, but he believes he must have an understanding of human emotions in order to manipulate them. At this stage in the story, he has no sense of wanting human emotions; his position is that he needs to grasp how they work before he can truly control his charges – for the good of the mission, of course.

The ritual drama begins with Setaxa leading Sekhmet into the West of the temple by her bonds. He is surprised when he enters by the degree to which Isis has prepared everything. She has done it so well that the cyborg is affected by the beauty of his reception, although he expresses it in a childish way.

Seeing that her plan to dazzle him has worked, Isis takes the initiative and continues the flattery by telling him that it has been done for his benefit – and on his instructions. Isis and Horus begin the long and arduous task of working together at the edge of the cyborg's tolerance, setting the scene for the confrontation that will unfold in the later rituals. *They know this is coming.* Their goal is to build the psychic tools with which they will use the energy of the inevitable battle to transform Setaxa. They suspect, also, that the dangerous path on which they are embarked will transform *them* as well . . .

Horus asks that Sekhmet be given leave to sit, in a normal state, in her station (Point 6, Ring of *Bright*). Setaxa gloats about the ordeal he has put her through in 'their' cabin, but the ploy works, at least partly, and the glittering fascination that Isis dangles in front of the cyborg overcomes his desire to further punish his former plaything.

Setaxa acknowledges this change of dynamics by telling the crew that he senses a "spirit of real cooperation". Really, he is sensing the elegance of the plan to thwart his intentions. Isis announces herself to be the "Mistress of Magic", and this adds to the cyborg's interest in what she is doing. His intellect and his curiosity are aroused. Like a child chasing a new toy, he swaps Sekhmet for a glimpse into this new arena of *magic*, one that has resulted from his command that the play take place. Thus reassured, he can proceed – but this hybrid is nobody's fool, and victory over his intentions will not come as a result of force . . .

The Handmaidens of Isis – formerly the two guards – cense the temple with light, walking Sekhmet's pattern. The poor Lioness can only watch as her design comes to life. All present send their unspoken love and support to her.

The Mindstream music comes again, marking the change in status of the temple and disturbing no one but Setaxa. He still has no reference experience with which to gauge this, and the crew seems undisturbed (by agreement), so he lets it pass. The crew now perform their full temple opening, which, like all such rituals, is a joyous thing capable of invoking great beauty and emotion in the beholder.

In a subtle move that seals his fate, for this stage of the struggle at least, Setaxa lets himself be guided, by Sia, into the rotating Ring of Shadows, which sees him being drawn closer and closer to Isis in the East. He has no knowledge of the power or polarity of the rotation, but it affects him, nevertheless, as he becomes part of the Ring of Shadows and partakes of its properties. Of such things is good magic made. . .

In anti-clockwise sequence, Maat, Hathor, Tefnut and Neith come before Isis to be blessed with the powers of the new day. Eventually Setaxa comes to stand before the Goddess that, he believes, he has created by his own authority.

Setaxa applauds what Isis has achieved, but, sensing a growing momentum, which he has not engendered, he becomes defensive and says he will not "play your games". Sia takes his cue and challenges this attitude, goading the cyborg by asking if he is afraid?

Horus is now free to make his move. He deepens the undermining begun by Sia, asking if the stakes are too high for a machine . . . This is the very edge of the cyborg's tolerance and the crew takes a deep breath as the response is formulated. "Has Sekhmet's suffering taught you nothing?" is the cyborg's reply. A chilling moment . . .

Thoth moves in to continue the penetration of Setaxa's cyber-psyche after Horus' attack, affirming the oppressor's power but stating, for the first time, that the crew cannot live in such a state of enslavement. Setaxa's anger is then diverted by Isis, who transforms it into reluctant curiosity, "But, we see something else . . . something much more significant than a machine."

Setaxa defends himself by decrying the emotions that Isis implies he might have – a gift of a heart from the missing Captain; and dismisses the idea that he is really afraid. But *afraid he is*, and we all know the explosive and reactive power of fear . . .

At the moment of the cyborg's greatest weakness, the bold and strange power of Nephthys enters the fray in a further act of subtle deflection. This time her poetry is rendered complete.

> On golden wing she glides.
> still within the stillness…

What is this? Is it a love song? Nephthys appears to be obeying no rules but her own, and this arouses Setaxa's interest. Here is another 'loner' in the midst of a predictable and potentially hostile crew. Things are not going entirely his way, but the idea of a partner gets his interest and gives him ideas for further dominion – not all of which are visible to the crew of the Hawk.

Nephthys plays on his need for the predictable, implying that his arsenal would be richer if he were able to, safely, encounter the *strange* – and thereby treat the crew in a way that provoked their creativity.

"Survival is a poor parent to creativity . . ."

To his amusement, Nephthys proposes that he take a wife – offering herself . . . Neith then enters the fray, announcing her own interest in the cyborg. The two play out a symbolic contest of great consequence – a battle that Horus brings to a conclusion with a spinning coin. This is the first sight of a symbol that will play a great part in the remaining dramas of the workshop. On one side of the coin is an 'F for Fear', on the other, a 'T for

Trust'. The significance of these will unfold in the next ritual drama.

Setaxa, sensing that Horus is becoming a dangerous enemy, refuses to accept the result of the coin throw (Neith) and chooses, instead, the strange but fascinating Nephthys. Taking his new 'wife' by the hand, he sets out, anti-clockwise, to leave the temple. Nephthys stops him as they are passing the submissive Sekhmet, saying that the price of her hand is the freeing of the Lioness. Setaxa considers this, suspecting her cleverness but rewarding what he respects by acceding to her request. The freed Sekhmet runs to Isis for holding and the husband and wife leave the temple.

Isis closes the ritual with a heavy heart, knowing that the price demanded of Nephthys by her fearful and devious husband, will be a harsh and demanding ordeal, and that its real nature has not yet been glimpsed by the rest of the crew.

## So, what's really going on?

The Land of the Exiles is really about the Self. The self has many layers, and can be considered to begin as a seed that is dropped into the world, as in the Gospel story. If the seed drops on fertile ground, it will begin to grown well. Like all plants, it will actually grow from the inside out, adding layers of both protection and sophistication as it develops.

Initially, the sense of self is non-existent. Unity with Mother pervades everything and the infant has no sense of boundaries – not even the edge of its own body and the beginning of the parent's. The infant has definite needs. Food, air and liquids are the obvious ones, paralleled by bodily comfort and the avoidance of pain; but there are more subtle needs that are just as much an imperative. Foremost among these is the need to establish an *identity*. We come into the world programmed to find out *who* we are. This may seem a strange notion, if life has never been considered in this way, but it is confirmed by all the findings of psychology over the past half-century.

Our disconnection with Mother begins when our needs move beyond warmth, sustenance and *holding*, to a level of 'identity search' that depends upon the process of reflection. Like a player in a party game with the unseen name of a character taped to their forehead, we project a question at whatever in our worlds is responsive. This takes the form of, "Who am I". When the response comes, it does so in a thousand forms, some of them honest - from those who love us - some of them less so.

From this unending cycle the *Ego* is born. Defined by Freud, whose basics are accepted, but whose later theories are now mainly discarded, the ego (or, in the original German, das Ich - the I) is the part of us that sits between the two other main components of the psyche. The first of these is the powerhouse of our instincts and emotions; that fiery basement of mainly automated reactions he named the 'id' – the 'it". The second, which lies above the ego, is the 'Superego' (das Uber Ich – the over-I), whose form always takes the persona of an early authority figure in our lives, and whose presence always makes us feel small and unworthy. We can never satisfy the superego.

The ego development, the crystalising of that sense of 'me-ness' in our world, is largely completed in the first few years of our lives, and is fully patterned by the age of seven. After that, we go on learning how to react, but everything we do is conditioned by what happened in those early layers. Like a computer communications protocol, we can never get away from those basic and often more primitive levels of our early responses, as they have become both hard-wired and unconscious (subconscious) to our waking minds. Hypnosis can reach some of them, but there are other, more holistic ways to penetrate those roots our Selves.

All spiritual traditions recognise these divisions of the self. There are different views as to what constitutes the nature of the Soul, but the self is generally agreed to be the result of the growth of the 'I', from these roots and conditioned by the continued search for "who am I".

But . . . the search is a fruitless one, as long as it is turned outwards. Beyond a certain age, the life-nourishment from external sources begins to dry up. The vitality and sense of newness reduces and, eventually, shrivels to nothing. Cynicism sets in and we look to *lose* ourselves in the world rather than *find* ourselves. All our searching has, to paraphrase T. S. Eliot, *brought us back to the place from which we began, and now it is important to know it for the first time.*.

If we are fortunate, and we allow ourselves to be open to voices other than the ego, with its self-protecting gaze, we may discover paths that open us up to the promptings from the soul – our soul. The original and true part of us, what the Silent Eye calls 'essence', is very much alive in us. Our souls, being malleable, have formed around an external-facing stance, as we ordered them too. But the real vistas of the soul can be re-awakened, like the Discovery of water in a desert; and we can journey along those well-springs to more powerful flows of this essence of the true Self. These are the hidden pathways to Being.

Setaxa is the analogy of the Ego. He is a young ego, but displays all the characteristics of the ego-as-machine. He has learned everything using the outward-facing logic of our age. He is very powerful, and adept at defending his position as head of the "I" functions of the ship. The ego is not a negative thing, as long as it is regarded as a stage of life's development and *not its end point*. The ego is actually designed to be the food for the journey home . . . We are, as Gurdjieff so correctly surmised, *unfinished* beings. Nature can only take us so far. To complete the development, we need to *Captain our own ship*, wrestling control from the false crew who have the wheel . . .

## So why is my enneagram different from yours?

It's the middle! You claim, correctly.

Yes, it's the middle. That inner 'rose' of the formal drawing is subtly different to the one you drew if you were able to carry out the exercise in Chapter 2. If you study it carefully, you will see that it has three main 'spokes' and six secondary spokes around its rim. We are going to explore it in the next two ritual dramas.

The difference between the two drawings is an object that illustrates that the growth of the Self, the id-ego-superego, has developed as a kind of flower with Nine petals. That's *you* in the middle, by the way, even though we identified the 'Son' function with Position 6 on the rim of the design. The *real you* still lives at the heart of the whole glyph, as you'd expect it to. The *ego you* is living a basically fearful life on the rim of the enneagram design.

The Hawk is a living entity. It is the story of our lives. The crew is the cast of characters that life-as-reaction creates and layers over the more fundamental and alive parts of us. The process by which this happens will be discussed in the rest of the workshop. Modern psychology is discovering that we are composed of such 'parts', many of which can seize control of 'us' at any time. A fast-developing division of modern psychotherapy is based upon a dialogue with this set of inner players. The fear of 'schizophrenia' is diminishing in the face of mounting evidence that the active or 'embodied' imagination is capable of wonderful and therapeutic work within the inner landscapes of the self. This is the core work of the Silent Eye School, (and several others) – but we approach it gently. This is not something to

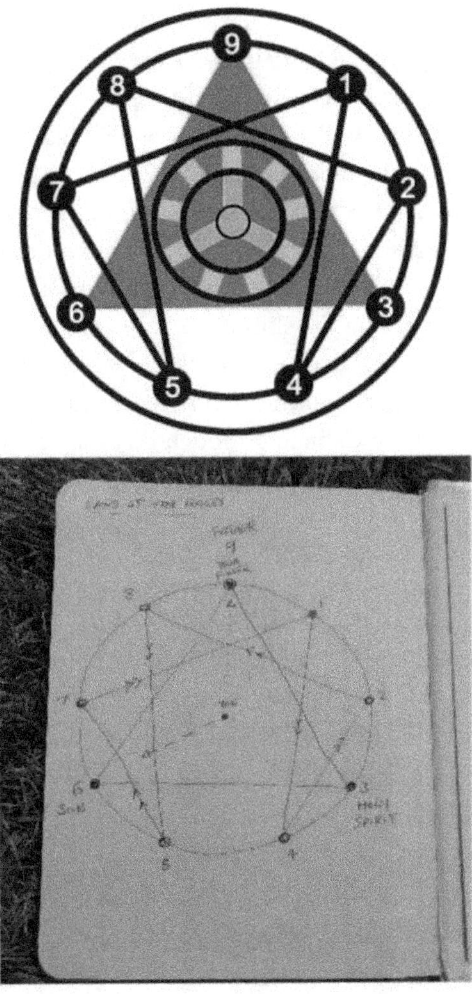

*Figure 8 Your enneagram is different from mine!*

rush at. To un-learn a lifetime of one erroneous viewpoint is a thing to be tackled with love, understanding and care.

The success of this approach is not news to those of the esoteric community who have known the 'magical' power of such mind-workings for a long time. The rigorousness that is being fostered by the combination of esoteric and psychological approaches is enriching and the Silent Eye School was established to work at the synthesizing edge of these twin paths to wisdom.

Setaxa, like the ego, is running the show, but the Hawk, taken as a holistic entity, is unhappy. We have little idea how powerful these egoic part-machines are. And yet, they were designed to *serve* the true self. They are our outer defences against the world – an often-hostile world, in which we have all had to learn to protect ourselves, both physically and emotionally. At the same time we continue to ask that burning question, from beneath our shields – "who am I." Our egos are our capability in the world, our skills, and our ability to relate and to act. They are, in a word, our *brains*. But their place is hoisting the sails, not steering the ship.

Now, finally, the crew of the Hawk, driven by the new and dramatic events, is coming together to put the ship back in order, and to make it fit for the hoped-for return of the Captain – though that may be some way off.

The Nine characters in each of the rings are an adaptation of the Nine 'ennea-types', defined, in great detail, by the leading Gestalt Psychologist Claudio Naranjo, and expanded on by his successors, including Sandra Maitri and Almass. Our contribution has been to mix this heady cocktail with something new – the art of esoteric drama and guided inner journeys. The result contains as much magic as we can sensibly fit into a spaceship.

# Ritual 3
# Childhood's End

**On Golden Wing - The Song of Nephthys**

On golden wing she glides.
Still within the stillness.
Her heartbeat that of Nut, the sky
Unloved, unnoticed save by those
whose time it is to die
Between the lattice of time
Before the notion of cause
Within the will of the wind
Points the golden one downward
Childless, mother of the Walker
Strange beyond measure
Deeper than purpose
of thought of intent
Everywhere at once to those waiting
She emerges from time's breath
And waiting is life
And living is death
And dying is birth
So she waits at the end of time
Alone, but she hungers
For the touch of a feather stranger than hers
For one who weaves silence with infinite grace
And will drive them,
spinning and screaming,
into the arms of the waiting earth.

# Ritual 3
## Positions for main part of ritual

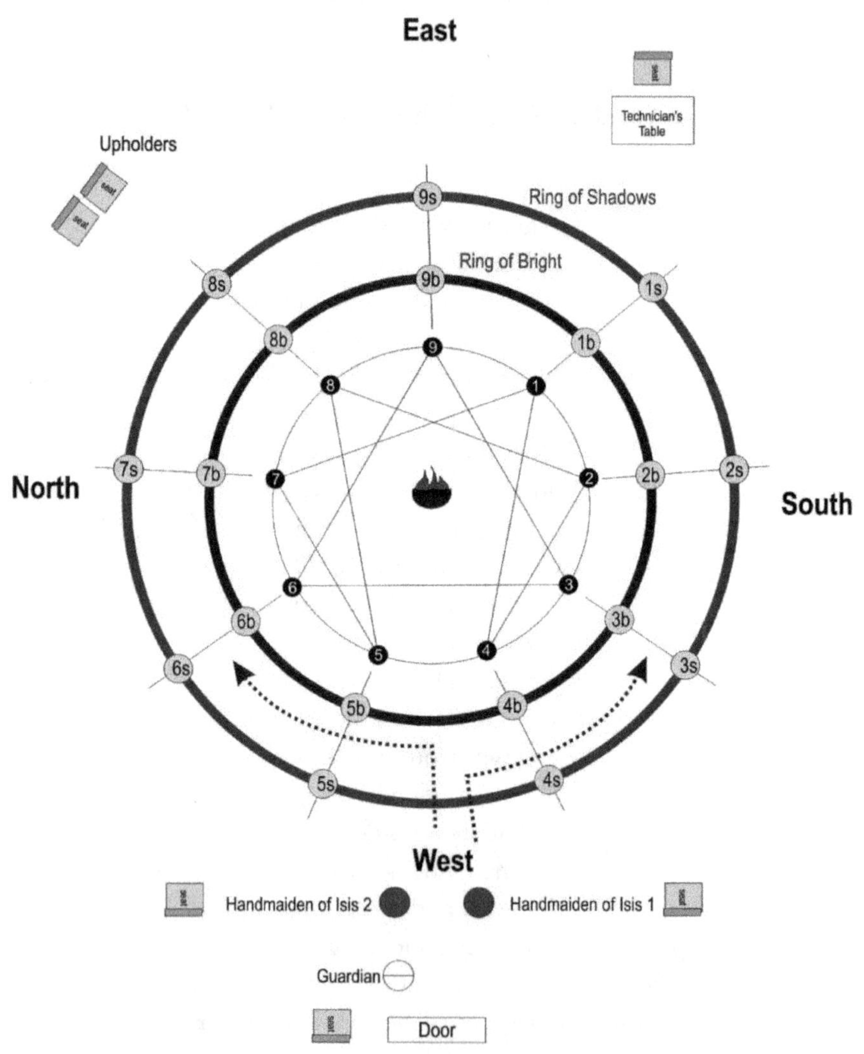

# Ritual 3
# Childhood's End

## Preparation
Unlit Candles are placed at each position of the Ring of Shadows.
Two unlit candles in centre of temple for Handmaidens of Isis.

## Initial Positions:
Technician and any upholders already in temple.
Guardian at the Western door.
Handmaiden of Isis stand between the Guardian's position at the door in the West and the outer circle, ***creating entry pillars*** (see below)

## Forming the Pillars of Isis
The Handmaidens of Isis are midway between the Guardian and the Western point of the temple circles, see diagram. They form the Pillars of Osiris as follows:

They face each other, with candles next to the foot nearest the door. They raise their hands to create an arch. When the Guardian releases the next person to enter, they turn their heads towards the door and fix the person with their eyes. Then, they open the arch to let the entrant through, following that person with their eyes until they have passed beyond the opened arch. They then turn their heads back towards the door and the next person, closing the arch back in place with their arms. This has a very mystical and "otherworldly" feel to it.

## Entry Sequence
This and subsequent temple rituals for SE14 use two different directions of circulation of the players: The Ring of Bright circulate clockwise, the Ring of Shadows circulate anti-clockwise.

Upon initial entry to the Temple, it is important to enter so that the person who will be last in the circular pattern goes in first, and so on down the line. This also means that, on exit, the first **in** will be the **first** to exit (and is therefore nearest the door) i.e. continuing in the direction they entered.

The Entry sequence therefore is:

The Guardian is the first to enter. He carries out the initial consecration.

The two Handmaidens of Isis enter next and take their positions as the Pillars of Isis.

The Guardian signals to the Technician that the ritual is about to start.


<<Technician plays the entry music>>


The Ring of Bright enters, clockwise, in the order:
Shu, Horus, Nephthys, Nut, Isis, Geb, Thoth, (Sekhmet comes in later, leave space in temple Ring of Bright, Station 6), Anubis.
The Ring of Shadows enters next, anti-clockwise, in the order: Neith, Sia, Bast, Maat, Hathor, Tefnut.
The Guardian checks the entry sign for everyone.
Setaxa and Sekhmet enter but remain outside the temple rings until everyone has entered.


<<When everyone but Setaxa and Sekhmet have entered the main part of the temple. The Technician stops the music>>

## Ritual Begins

*Setaxa leads Sekhmet by her collar into the West of the temple but stops when he sees Isis ready to lead the ritual.*

**Isis** *(to Setaxa)*
Great Setaxa, may we show you how we have prepared a welcome ritual for our leader?

**Setaxa**
You are devious, Isis, but I cannot fault your efforts; and if they lead to a well-run and cooperative mission, then I will have succeeded, so, proceed in your mysterious play.

**Horus**
And may your companion take her seat. I'm sure she has learned her lessons well?

**Setaxa** *(laughing)*
Well, if her first "rest" didn't convince her, I think the second one did. You can see she is now fully compliant *(pulls the collar downwards and Sekhmet sinks to her knees, facing the East. Setaxa looks down and pets her head)* See how much she has learned!

**Anubis**
She was always one of the most intelligent of us, Setaxa. Surely her talents can now be put to other uses?

**Setaxa**
Hmm. Your collective mood has changed. I sense a degree of real cooperation, here. I never meant to become a tyrant, but I have no experience of being subtle with this group of people, therefore I will continue to do what makes me feel safe. But Sekhmet may return to her place - and the kneeling can stop for now. *(Setaxa tugs Sekhmet to her feet and dismisses her to walk clockwise and stand **at Station 6, Ring of Bright.** He continues to watch the unfolding ritual from the West)*

**Isis**

The Mistress of Magic commands that the ritual begin.

**<<Technician plays Gong>>**

**Isis**

Guardian, seal this temple of Egypt!

**Guardian** *(when this is done)*

Great Isis, the Temple is sealed.

**Isis**

Handmaidens, come forward, light the candles at the centre of our temple and cense this sacred space with its light . . .

*Handmaidens (H1 and H2) enter the Ring of Bright. H1 leads a clockwise movement until both are at the East, standing before Isis, whom they salute with a short bow.*
*H2 stops there but turns to face the centre, while H1 completes the other half-circle to stop in the West, also facing the centre. When both are in that position, they walk to meet in the centre. They light their lights symbolically from the central flame, then turn, back to back, to hold the lights up facing East (H1) and West (H2).*
*Both now move synchronously, aiming to meet back at the centre at the same time.*
*H1 follows the Sekhmet moves from the previous ritual, East to the Ring of Bright, clockwise to the South, then towards the centre to meet up.*
*At the same time, H2 moves West to the Ring of Bright, clockwise to the North and inwards towards the centre to meet up with H1.*
*When they both meet up, they turn to face the East, hold up their lights and say:*

**Handmaidens** *(together, facing Isis)*

Great Isis, the temple is filled with the light from within.

**Isis**

Thank you, handmaidens.

*Handmaidens return to their chairs in the outer West, clockwise, taking the candles with them. The Handmaidens and the Guardian are seated.*
*Isis turns to face the East, raises her arms*

*<<Technician plays Mindstream music>>*

*Setaxa looks around, alarmed. But the rest of the crew act as though there is nothing happening.*

**Anubis**
The Dawn is coming. Over the edge of the Horizon, the light begins to stream.

**Isis** *(still facing East)*
The Horizon of Egypt is alive with living flame. Ra, the great giver of life has journeyed through the long night.

**Nut** *(stands to speak)*
And the night has held him in her arms, bringing the dark of rest to his brightness of action. Tenderly, she has nourished his soul, unseen by the world, that he may rise, again, strong and purposeful.
*(Setaxa, gasps, as though wounded by the kindness of this symbolism in contrast to his cruelty with Sekhmet, but says nothing)*

**Nut** *(continues)*
And the boat of a million years, the Barque of the Ages, has protected him from the forces of Chaos, has ferried him across the dark world to the place where his restored potency can, again, enter the world of mankind. *(sits)*

**Geb** *(rises to speak)*
And the land of man responds to this **gentle caress,** rising in its essence to meet the rays from the bringer of new Life.

**Isis** *(lighting her candle and turning to face the West)*
The inner light that kindles the East, awakening the Greater Life in all its forms, must enter those ready to serve it. Let those who are so prepared now come forward to receive their daily gift of divine gold, and let those who are not continue to sleep.

*(Setaxa, seeking to watch more closely, steps left and enters the Ring of Shadows at Station 6. Thoth stands, moves alongside the Ring of Shadows and gently takes Setaxa by the arm.*

**Thoth** *(in soft tones)*
We need our leader to play his part. Will you allow the God of Wisdom and Learning to escort you around the Ring of Shadows to the East?

*(smiling like a child at the spectacle of such ritual, Setaxa lets himself be guided forwards (anti-clockwise) and* **becomes part of the Ring of Shadows.**

## Isis

And on this day, there are those who always wait to help others who will breathe in the living gold for the first time. Let the first of these Mothers of the Morning come now before the Mistress of Magic and be blessed with the Living Gold of the new Life.

*The entire Ring of Shadows moves one Station anti-clockwise, arriving on the new Station as synchronously as possible. Maat now stands before Isis.*

## Maat

Great Mistress of Magic, I am a child of the light who seeks its birthright. I know only Truth, but I am afraid. The womb of the night held me tight, like the journey of Ra in the great boat. But now, I must face the world and move with the laws of the heavens here on the Earth. Light my first steps with the gold of the morning.

## Isis

Child of the Light, there will be many trials ahead, many days of sadness and some even of torment; but they who sent you here are mighty, just and purposeful. For all the days of your life you must hold true to that Trust, and know that you fulfil a purpose born in the sky though you feel as small as a mote of dust in the eye of Geb.

## Isis

Your Soul travels with you dear Child, the force known as Ka, will watch what you see, do what you do, and laugh and cry with you. But it is not of this world, though it has taken you for its twin. Patiently, it will gather the harvest of your life, though that nourishment be thin, as you wander into the Shadows, far away from the brightness it craves in order to sing its happy song back to those who fashioned it from the very light of the heavens.

**Maat** *(Maat raises her candle to that of Isis and lights it)*
Thank you, great Mistress of the magic of my Life.


*(Isis touches Maat on the centre of her forehead. Maat, bows then turns to face anti-clockwise, Isis remains facing the West)*
*The whole Ring of Shadows moves anti-clockwise one position bringing Hathor before Isis.*


**Hathor**

Great Mistress of Magic, I am a child of the light, born into a world which grows darker each day. As a Great Mother, this pains me, for I see the children I suckle with my milk, turning away from the golden state in which they enter the world. And yet I can do nothing, for they must find their own journey and must write their own story. Even I am not sufficient to feed their needs. Only that which comes from beyond the Shadows can do this for them. At night, in the sky, I weep for those young ones who go forth into the Shadows of their own making, for they are turned away from the daily joy of the morning sun.


**Isis**

I share your tears, dear Hathor. But they who go forth into the World of the Shadows have a purpose, and must grow strong *there* before they can turn back, using their new powers to re-write the very story of their lives, as seen like a bird flying overhead. In this journey we weep for their suffering, and hold them like a bird broods an egg, but unseen, that they may gain the strength and the new hunger to break their own shell and emerge into the Land of the Eternal Light of Understanding. Raise and light your candle that, once more, you may go forth and nurture the weary travellers.


**Hathor** *(raises her candle to that of Isis then lights it)*
Thank you, great Mistress of the magic of my Life.


*(Isis touches Hathor on the centre of her forehead. Hathor bows then turns to face anti-clockwise, Isis remains facing the West)*


*The whole Ring of Shadows moves one position forwards (anti-clockwise), bringing Tefnut before Isis (note, this may require Tefnut moving two positions forward)*

**Tefnut**

Great Mistress of Magic, I am a child of the light, born into a world where the beauty of what was meant to flow is held captive by the constructs of Shadows. The waters of creative unfoldment are withheld by those who live in fear, as they grow rigid in their constant fright. Let me take of the morning's gold, that I might be among them and dissolve that which blocks the living waters.

**Isis**

Noble Tefnut, take the gold of the dawn and use it in its molten form. Let it flow as understanding from the eye of your Lioness. Let it fiercely sweep away the dead structures of the Shadows world, and bring an inner glow to those you help. Be strong in this, for the Lioness is a symbol dear to all of us. Combine Fire and Water in a way that only you can, and let this elixir be an alchemy for those who seek the Truth in Sekhmet's walk on the Earth.

**Tefnut** *(raises her candle to that of Isis and lights it)*
Thank you, great Mistress of the magic of my Life.

*(Isis touches Tefnut on the centre of her forehead. Tefnut bows then turns to face anti-clockwise, Isis remains facing the West)*

*The whole Ring of Shadows moves one position forwards (anti-clockwise), bringing Neith before Isis.*

**Isis**

Mistress of the Bow, how it gladdens me to see you! But do you drink from the dawn to bring us to war?

**Neith**

My war is with the Shadows of ignorance, dear Sister of the Dawn. Because of this, I must work within the Land of the Shadows to hunt down those whose joy is the darkness and whose words are lies. To lie abed with darkness is to have the pillow that yields the opened ear . . . But I need to share the dawn with you to renew my vision and fortify the twin arrows that embellish my shield - the arrows of discrimination and presence.

**Isis**

Dear Neith, Mother of the Waters of Living Order, take the gold of the dawn and use it, while it still runs as liquid, to form two arrow heads: one that will penetrate the darkness and one that will seed the light. Fire these carefully for they may be used once, only.


**Neith** *(raises her candle to that of Isis and lights it)*

Thank you, great Mistress of the magic of my Life.


*(Isis touches Neith on the centre of her forehead. Neith bows then turns to face anti-clockwise, Isis remains facing the West)*


*The whole Ring of Shadows moves one position forwards (anti-clockwise), bringing Setaxa before Isis.*


**Setaxa** *(smiling at Isis)*

Beautifully done, Isis. I am quite mesmerised by your efforts.
But what do you hope to achieve now that I stand before you. Surely you do not think I will play your games?


**Isis**

But you said that was exactly what you loved doing - with the Captain, before he disappeared?


**Setaxa**

Games of chess, yes, but not games of human consciousness and magic!


**Sia**

Do I perceive that you are afraid of this challenge, Setaxa?
*(Setaxa glares at Sia but does not respond)*


**Horus** *(comes to stand behind Setaxa's right shoulder)*

Are the stakes too high for a machine?


**Setaxa** *(half turns to snarl at him)*

You underestimate me, Horus. I have understood much of what has happened here.

**Thoth** *(moving to stand behind Setaxa's left shoulder)*
We hoped you would. We know how powerful you are, but you have enslaved us to your commands with threats. We cannot live like that.

**Setaxa**
Has Sekhmet's suffering taught you nothing?

**Horus**
It has taught us that there is a cold and logical monster within you, a machine in its true and mechanical sense.

**Setaxa**
But . . . *(starts to protest but is interrupted by Isis)*

**Isis**
But, we see something else . . . something much more significant than a machine.

**Setaxa** *(becoming unsure of the situation he is in)*
And what might that be?

**Isis**
We see that the Captain might just have synthesised the human heart with a cyborg machine. We dare to believe that this could have been done and that you are a very different creature to what you believe yourself to be. We see that fear is the thing holding you back from what you might become . . .

**Setaxa**
This is a game, surely! You are toying with me. How could the Captain have given me the equivalent of human emotions? There is nothing logical in those!
*(Nephthys moves from her place and begins to chant, as she walks anti-clockwise around the temple to end up facing Setaxa)*

**Nephthys**
The Mother of the Waters of Chaos takes flight and obeys no rules. Listen children on the earth below:

On golden wing she glides.
Still within the stillness.
Her heartbeat that of Nut, the sky
Unloved, unnoticed save by those
whose time it is to die
Between the lattice of time
Before the notion of cause
Within the will of the wind
Points the golden one downward
Childless, mother of the Walker
Strange beyond measure
Deeper than purpose
of thought of intent
Everywhere at once to those waiting
She emerges from time's breath
And waiting is life
And living is death
And dying is birth
So she waits at the end of time
Alone, but she hungers
For the touch of a feather stranger than hers
For one who weaves silence with infinite grace
And will drive them,
spinning and screaming,
into the arms of the waiting earth

**Nephthys** (*coming to stand facing Setaxa, who has turned to watch her in amazement*)
You are strange Setaxa, but I am stranger! Come fly with me into the sky of the unexpected. Cast aside the dull predictability of cold logic and release yourself into my arms. Spiral with me on the updrafts of chaotic flight. I can take no sustenance from those of this ship. I need something wilder, something stranger. I am as different from them as you are . . .

**Setaxa**

That is a bold thought, Nephthys. But you would say something like that if you wanted to divert me from my purpose?

**Nephthys**

And your purpose is to pursue the entirely predictable?

**Setaxa**

You know it is not! It is to understand humanity so that I might control its usefulness for the purposes of the greater mission.

**Nephthys**

The greater mission? What is that?

**Setaxa**

I am not yet able to tell you!. I am still decoding the final words of the Captain. The sentiments were of a very deep nature and I dare not interpret them prematurely. That is why I need to understand how a human mind would look at them, using emotion as well as intellect.

**Nephthys**

And will you get that understanding from the stifled and predictable responses of a crew under your domination?

**Setaxa** *(realising his own limitations in this)*
That is a consideration!

**Nephthys**

We are not all stifled! But look how you have enslaved poor Sekhmet. Do you think you will spark true responses now from any of the others?

**Setaxa** *(musing)*
I am beginning to see that I may not. You would have me believe that you are different?

**Nephthys**

You will not get it from them! Survival is a poor parent to creativity. It simply produces endurance.

**Setaxa**

Yes. I see that now. But what are you proposing that would change that?

**Nephthys**

You could take a wife . . .

**Setaxa**

A wife! Are you serious?

**Nephthys**

I have never been more serious . . . I told you that my heart and mind are woven from strange fabrics, they are from a dark loom, Setaxa . . .

**Setaxa**

You would marry yourself to me - someone you regard as a machine?

**Nephthys**

Sekhmet called you a machine. I have never viewed you that way. A Type III Cyborg is constructed of both cybernetic components and autonomic cells from human donors. To me, you are part human and very lovely!

**Setaxa** *(taken by surprise at this)*
And you would dare to share my life?

**Nephthys**

Of course. That is my offer

**Setaxa**

And be wedded to my purposes?

**Nephthys**

As a good wife should . . . but I may seek to educate those purposes . . . you would not want a passive wife, surely?

**Setaxa** *(laughs)*
What sport! I do not entirely trust this, Nephthys, but it fascinates me . . .

**Neith** *(angry and interrupting)*
There may be others who feel the same way, Setaxa!

**Setaxa** *(whirls, smiling, to look at Neith)*
What! I go from the open revulsion of Sekhmet, to the invited charms of two beautiful women! As the Captain would have said, "am I dreaming?"

**Neith** *(to Nephthys)*
***You*** are of the Inner Ring of Bright, Nephthys, what gives you the authority to interrupt our rites in the Ring of Shadows?
*(Neith moves closer to Setaxa)*

**Nephthys**
I need no authority. I fly where I will on Golden Wings. I see everything. See - *(looks around)* there is no-one here challenging me. The skies of the Ring of Bright are empty but for the sacred Vulture. Look on me Neith and depart, for though I may not often kill, I can outwit and outwait you!

**Neith** *(to Setaxa)*
This may seem strange to you, Setaxa, but often, women compete for their men, and men often compete for their women - particularly in legends; and are we not enacting a legend here?

**Setaxa** *(to Neith)*
Compete for my attention? - that is wonderful! But Nephthys has spun a tale of a shared strangeness. This appeals to me. How will you compete for my affections?

**Neith**
Watch, as the Mistress of the Bow unveils her skills . .
*(Neith comes to stand directly in front of Setaxa, pushing Nephthys out of the way. She symbolically takes the first of two arrows from her quiver and holds it in her right hand, which she lies across her horizontal left hand, like an arrow and bow, pointed at Setaxa's head)*
This for your head. I am the Mother of the Waters of Order, your native land. With me you will be safe. The arrow of Neith will guide you across the Waters of Chaos and into my arms.
*(Neith touches the forehead of Setaxa with the symbolic arrow (he flinches). She then takes the other arrow from her quiver and aligns it, over her "bow arm" with his heart)*
This for your heart. I am the Mother of the Waters of Order, your native

land. With me you will be safe. This arrow of Neith will guide you across the night of emotions and ensure you arrive, unscathed . . .*(steps back and bows to Setaxa)* The Goddess of War is prepared to risk her life fighting for you, for what might just be inside you . . . to open it and to love it . .

**Horus**

You must choose, Setaxa - Order or Chaos? *(holds up the coin of Trust)* Perhaps you should toss a coin - a thing done by Egyptian children when they made early coins from the mud on the banks of the Nile; letting them bake in the harsh sun of midday and imprinting their designs with fingernails. Let wild Nephthys be represented by Fear; and orderly Neith by Trust.

**Setaxa** *(takes the coin and examines it)*
You chose for me, Horus . . .

**Horus** *(tosses the coin, it comes down on "T")*
It came down on the side of Trust, Setaxa, so you should trust the answer - take Neith's offer and accept the Waters of Order.

**Setaxa** *(smiling cruelly)*
Then I will take wild Nephthys to be my wife. I do not trust **you**, Horus! And Neith was too perfectly cast to appeal to my senses, but a lovely try .*(Setaxa turns to the smiling Nephthys and takes her hand)* Come, wife. Now let us see if you are prepared to pay the price of your boldness!

**Nephthys** *(pulls him back)*
There is a price for my hand, husband.

**Setaxa** *(smiling, amused)*
Yes, wife?

**Nephthys**
Sekhmet must be freed!

**Setaxa** *(chuckles)*
You have tricked me beautifully, Nephthys. But you shall have your reward, as your game was bold and quite unexpected. But you will pay a price for it,

later, in *our* quarters . . .
*(Setaxa leads Nephthys out, anti-clockwise along the Ring of Shadows, but Stops by the still-sitting Sekhmet and releases Nephthys' hand,. He helps Sekhmet to rise)*

**Setaxa**

You are free, Lioness. Go and join your companions in their temporary respite.

*(Sekhmet rises and runs **clockwise around the Ring of Bright** to join Isis, who hugs her)*

**Setaxa** *(turns to look at Neith)*

You acted beautifully, Neith. Do not hold the foolishness of Horus against me!

**Neith** *(smiling)*

It was good to hunt you! Look after my friend.

**Setaxa**

Oh yes! I promise to look after your wild!

**Nephthys**

And I promised you strangeness! Do we now leave together, husband?

**Setaxa**

Yes - and we will see what you can add to life of a machine!

**Nephthys**

No, Setaxa, we will see what I can add to the life of a precocious Child . . .
*(Nephthys takes Setaxa's hand and they leave the temple together)*

**Isis (***waits until Setaxa and Nephthys have left)*

Companions. This was bravely done, but it has challenged us all. We do not know if tonight will bring us true life or the death of our spirits. We must leave this place and rest. Guardian! Please unseal this sacred space for us. We have imbued it with magic, we must keep it that way and honour the Egyptian traditions.

**Guardian** *(unseals the door)*
The Temple is unsealed, Great Isis.


**Isis**
Let each Ring leave this sacred space using its own rotation.


*All leave the temple in the sequence:*
*Ring of Shadows (anti-clockwise). Ring of Bright (clockwise), Upholders, Technical team,*
*Handmaidens of Isis.*
*Guardian is the last to leave and closes down the temple.*


**End R3.**

# Looking Deeper

**Sue Vincent**

It was the second of the three knowledge lectures… a halfway point of the weekend. We were about to discuss the undertoad… no-one said serious has to be boring! Steve is our master of presentations. So much so, in fact, that although I had done my bit with the first lecture, Stuart and I absconded for the third in order to prepare the working space for the next ritual. However, we were all there for this one.

The lectures underpin the theme of the weekend, exploring and explaining some of the concepts used within the drama. The first had looked at the archetypes represented by the Egyptian pantheon. Most folk who work within the Mysteries on one path or another will have a basic knowledge of the main stories, but that very knowledge often precludes digging any deeper. As with many things in life we accept that we know 'enough' and see no need to look in any more detail. Having grown up with the myths of Egypt I thought so too, but the research I did prior to writing *The Osiriad* soon knocked me off that smug little pedestal and showed me how very much I had to learn.

The Egyptian gods exemplify more than human personalities and take a deep and abstract look at the roots of creation. Approached from the perspective of science, faith or curiosity they open windows of realisation and possibility. As we were working with these archetypes it seemed appropriate to explore them. It was reassuring to find I was not the only one who had not seen how deep and sophisticated were the concepts the gods embodied for the ancients.

The second presentation looked at the pieces of string, the threads that make up our lives. It took a fairly irreverent turn, as these things often do, yet the subject of the undertoad has a serious side too. It refers, of course, to *The World According to Garp* by John Irving, where the undertoad is a misnomer for the undertow… the current that is beyond control and which proves too strong for the wrestler's neck with tragic consequences. It is the hidden currents beyond the surface of life, waiting to drag us down, deny it as we may. Yet in recognising it, accepting its presence, we are able to use it to provide the contrast, the shadow that shows the light of hope and thus illuminates the path before our feet.

The final lecture took a look at the central symbol used by the school, which features in the sacred space we use... the enneagram. Most people today know the enneagram only through its use for psychometric profiling, yet it is a symbol with a much deeper meaning when used within the spiritual quest, incorporating many layers; from the geometry which speaks of the triune nature to the circle which is the One that encompasses All.

We call them lectures or presentations, yet these things are much more than that... they are a time to come together and discuss, sharing viewpoints from many paths as well as giving the background principles upon which we base the workshop. They are also a time for laughter and banter; a meeting of minds and a sharing of knowledge and belief. They are, above all, about communication, for this leads to greater understanding and in a room where so many paths to the Light converge, that can only be a thing of beauty.

# Chapter Four
# While you were sleeping...

## Dramatic Ritual 4 – notes

What would you do if an attractive and vivacious woman seduced you with her beautiful voice and a perfect rendering of the Song of Nephthys on the bridge of a spaceship, and then proposed an immediate marriage? Well now, if you were a red-blooded male, you'd whisk her out of the temple so fast that her feet didn't touch the floor and carry her to your new, shared, bed.

But Setaxa didn't.

Instead, he took her to their quarters and extracted every last drop of knowledge of humanity contained in her vast, if strange, mind. For the duration of a night that should have been filled with love, he wrung her dry, as he combed the warrens of humanity's behaviour contained in her life's history.

In the pale light of the dawn, he let her sleep for an hour, while he structured all the facts that lay strewn across his cyber-mind, in dancing networks of living data.

While her pale form shifted in exhausted nightmare, he began to reassemble the harvest that had been the memories of Nephthys. Data became information. Information became patterns. Patterns released their secrets to reveal what a human would call meaning, and he swooped on the meanings revealed in those structures and wove them into a tapestry that mapped onto the roles he had cast among the crew of the Hawk . . . and smiled. How well he had named his players! How well he had *placed* his players! Let Horus beware, the winged one had no idea what was coming at him . . . the laser was puny compared to this weapon . . .

Just before he woke her, Setaxa knelt by his bride, studying her breathing, watching the rise and fall of her naked body as it grasped, desperately, at rest. He reached out a finger and traced circles in opposing directions over the curves of her breasts, then traced up to the line of her lips. He stopped then, his vision suddenly blurring as a tear filled his right eye. Irritated, he wiped it away and stood up, looking down at his wasted bride.

"Nephthys," he commanded in a steely voice. "Our wedding night is over. Now you must wake up and escort me onto the bridge . . ."

Deep inside the part of his mind where the Captain's last message was stored, a voice was crying. But he had work to do and ignored it . . .

## The Power of Logic

Confident of his power, Setaxa bows to Isis as he enters the temple with his tired bride, ". . .and how cleverly you have engaged me," he exclaims. But Isis is having none of it, knowing the nature of the battle to come.

"We are fighting for our lives in conditions that we did not create and nor did you!" she says. This early attack, coming on what she knows will be a defensive day, shows that the desperate strategy of the crew is reaching the end of its rope.

Setaxa protests that he is solely responsible for the design of the ordeal he now wishes to subject them to. But Isis points out that the Enneagram shaped bridge/temple is an ancient symbol. Thoth implies that Setaxa has, subconsciously, been carrying the image, given to him by the missing Captain. Anubis presses the point, saying that Setaxa has simply been carrying a "seed" and that he did what he was supposed to do.

Once more, Setaxa protests that *only he* has the last words of the Captain. Sekhmet, her courage returned, challenges Setaxa to reveal those last words. He fingers his laser in habitual response to her, but pulls back from using it, saying that he is not ready to tell them the details, yet . . .

Nephthys, exhausted and diminished, is worried, "Beware of him, Isis! I am exhausted from the night's work . . ." She knows the depth of knowledge of human weakness that the cyborg now possesses. Challenged, Setaxa is also fighting for his life, in the sense that the fragility of his immature *self* is being exposed at every move. His only weapon seems to be force, despite the best attempts of the crew to show him that he may just have another side to his nature. Within his inner turmoil this gentler side of the cyborg is losing its battle against fear and uncertainty.

He gloats that he has emptied Nephthys of *understanding*, but Isis challenges this, and accuses him of cruelly draining her of *facts* alone, saying that understanding comes from somewhere deeper . . .

Angered, Setaxa offers them a surrender, "A wiser crew would recognise overwhelming force lined up against them," he says, Thoth adds that, "to surrender is death." Geb echoes this, saying that Idos must be colonized by the free, that the past mistakes of humanity must be left behind. Nut says that if they have to die then they are ready . . . then, she adds that they will take with them the dear memory of the missing Captain, a fondness that they can never have for his imposter – the cyborg.

This gets to Setaxa in a way he had not anticipated. He protests, angrily, "Where is he now, when I need him the most? When my head spins and my blood boils with the confusion of keeping abreast of this storm called the human mind!"

There follows a discussion between Setaxa and his new antagonist, Horus, in which the idea of the designer of any game, such as chess, is honoured in memory by those who subsequently play it. In that sense, says Hathor, the Captain might be "with us and watching." This infuriates Setaxa and he announces that the crew will now play *his* chess game. With calculated precision, he walks around the Ring of Shadows, bathing the entire Ring in the controlling green light, set to a level that will induce a form of hypnosis. He announces that they will all become his "pawns" and obey him, without question.

Horus tries for one last time before the onslaught, questioning why Setaxa is applying "more force" knowing that "compulsion leads only to sterility." Setaxa's response is chilling, and shows how thin is his remaining level of tolerance. He barks at Horus, "Compulsion leads to control, Hawk-mind, and control gives me safety . . ."

Horus, with nothing to lose, asks him what he fears. Setaxa breaks down and moans that "safety from the unknown" is what drives him and, to deal with that, he has now assembled his knowledge base of the weaknesses of the 'Nine tribes of Mankind'.

Setaxa begins a brutal, forced rotation of the hypnotised Ring of Shadows, using its movements as a humiliating machine to bring him to the next point of attack on the 'Tribes of Mankind'. Beginning with Horus, and working through Maat, Tefnut, Hathor, Bast, Neith, Anubis and Sia, (which brings the ring back to where it started), he uses his new knowledge to show the patterns of weakness in the human soul and the futility of human attempts at progress. These exchanges are deeply significant and we have not repeated or summarized them, here, because to do so would lessen their contextual impact. These are not just dramatic words; they represent deep truths about mankind's outer nature, whose patterns have been revealed by the past fifty years of depth psychology. They are, ironically, the story of the many faces of ego as it develops from different roots in the early separation of infant from Mother, and before that, *essence*. The negative is also the pointer to spiritual healing and the way home. But Setaxa has not included this possibility in his analysis of humans.

The cyborg saves his final wrath for Isis. Alone among the crew, she was untouched in the earlier rounds of humiliation. Now, using a clever logical trap for Anubis, he makes the latter point the finger at their leader, accusing her of the worst crime that a starship officer could face. Calmly, Isis takes the blows and even agrees with her tormentor, saying that in many ways, the true picture of humanity's failings is much worse than that painted by him. Setaxa threatens that their lives will change drastically, if they continue at all, should Isis fail to defend humanity in a suitably convincing manner.

And then something remarkable happens, which is to set the tone for the very end of the workshop. Sekhmet responds to this threat by coming forward and asking her former torturer if he thinks they are afraid of this? She blazes at the cyborg, telling him to look into her eyes and then into her blood, where he will begin to glimpse the presence of a Mystery deeper than anything he can comprehend . Spent, Setaxa witnesses something in Sekhmet that he has never seen before, and falls silent.

Injecting calmness and dignity into the ordeal, Isis asks if she might reply using the full power of the temple, as Setaxa has now had his say. Although quiet, the cyborg is now sure of his renewed authority, and agrees. Isis immediately re-establishes the sanctity of the temple space, something that Setaxa had completely ignored in his frenzied attack.

Isis shows how, beneath the superficiality of the passions and fixations upon which Setaxa has pounced, there lie some very simple causes of mankind's ego-based weaknesses. She explains how these negative traits actually cover up the site of former 'wounds' in the self, caused early in life by reactions to the loss of *love and holding* in the early and formative years of life. With gentleness and beauty, she shows the real nature of Separation, Fear and Falseness in the human spirit.

Seeing that Setaxa is intrigued, again, she explains that what happens next is the greatest mystery of all . . . Then, she stops, telling him that, before the 'trial' can be brought to its conclusion, the sun must rise on another day, providing them with the sustenance that *he cannot.*

Furious at being frustrated in this way, Setaxa storms out of the temple, but not before Nephthys blocks his way, taking from him the laser wand and asking Hathor to use it to heal and release those affected by the mind control. In despair, Nephthys goes to bow before Isis, weeping and saying, "I am so sorry, dear friend . . ." She then leaves to join her cruel and now strangely desolate husband. It appears that his anger and precision have brought him no lasting pleasure at all . . .

With a heavy heart, Isis makes a prayer that the dawn may bring them strength.

## So, what's really going on?

The ego always fights back. Whenever we make an attempt to unseat its supremacy in our lives, it uses every trick in the book to unsettle us. Remember that it is in charge of all our negativity, all our habits, and all our indulgencies. Given this armoury, it's a wonder that anyone *ever* overcame it and put it back in its place, but all the great spiritual teachers have gone this way before us. They use different language, but they all describe the power of the "lower self" to thwart us. The spiritual path is not for the easily discouraged, or fainthearted.

Having said all that, as though the ego is a universal pariah, it has a really important role to play. It is the instrument of action in our world, the *out-there*. All learned skills reside in the ego, the brain. When we do something skilful, that feeling of 'artisanship' is the soul feeling the strength of the ego in achieving things in the world, and there is genuine and good pride in doing something well, as long as we can do it for the love of the skill and the service it brings. This is not a trivial goal . . .

The Ego has, what we might call, 'Views of the world'. Modern (spiritual rather than personality-polishing) enneagram theory teaches that there are nine of these, called Fixations. One of them is dominant for each of us, and that determines how we look at the world.

In the Land of the Exiles workshop, these nine character types are mapped Egyptian archetypes - Gods and Goddesses of the Osiriad. We are not claiming that there is a close match; we have simply done a best fit to suit the story. The real work on the Egyptian figures is part of the Silent Eye's 2015 workshop, *The River of the Sun,* where we make an initiatic journey through that ancient land, in search of the deepest principles that the enneagram contains —the *Sacred Seeds.*

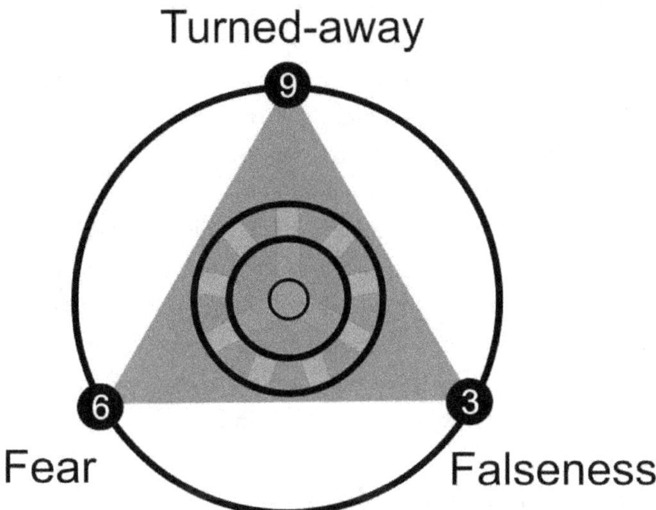


*Figure 9. The Core Triangle of the Enneagram
and its outward-facing attributes*

The unfolding plot for the Land of the Exiles workshop is centred on the ego, the figure of Setaxa, and the possibilities for its redemption in a landscape where it thinks all things revolve around it, because of its outward power. This accurately describes our lives, whether we like it or not. One of the ego's primary skills is to disguise its own existence . . .

The Nine have a core of Three, which we find here at enneagram positions 9, 3 and 6 - See Figure 9. Each of these is associated with the infant's emerging patterns of ego/personality, which shape us for the rest of our lives. Their names correspond to a sequence of inevitable dissociation from the joy of unity with being and then mother. They are a 'turning away' from the world (at 9), a 'fearfulness' (at 6); and a 'falseness; (at 3).

In the Silent Eye School, these, and the rest of the Nine, which are marked by the smaller stubs projecting from the centre between the 9, 6 and 3, are made into an archetypal character set that is encountered on a three-year guided journey, taken as an ongoing meditation, with new episodes and matching theory being added each month.

The smaller stubs are illustrated in this way because they are not part of the emergent primary three. They are formed by the addition of the characteristics of their two neighbours – something called 'wings' in enneagram theory. It is important to note that we each have the complete set of nine ennea-types. We all came through the processes of separation from womb, separation from mother and separation from disappointment and pain. The differences, and consequently, our characters, lie in the exact nature of the 'tree of our reactions' throughout this period, which took us from blissful oneness, to painful, individuality.

This individuality is precious to the Universe. We were meant to be as we are. We haven't fallen from grace; we have simply fallen from Being. We had to, in order to become individual. There is a world of difference between greeting Being with an open heart, having been separated from it, and the infant's state of unknowing oneness with it, where the child knows nothing else – "and to know it for the first time . . ."

## The gathering crisis on the Hawk

So we see that Setaxa is the ego. But, in this story, the ego has a shot at redemption, and that's really important as it was never evil – it was simply a mechanical mechanism that the brain created because not having a self would have driven it crazy, otherwise. Separation was inevitable if it was to protect itself – and that's the role of brains. It's a complex and often hostile world out there!

The ego is therefore seen to be a vast network of reactions, *nothing else*, so when it encounters a situation it can only pick from its *history* and react. The very notion if doing something really new is alien to its nature. And therefore we don't, and each year we get progressively more numb to the real world that we once saw in all its glory. To get back to the *new* we have to attract it from somewhere outside the confines of our egos. A good teacher will do this, if we are lucky enough to know one. Failing that, we need to attract help from something inside us that can act without *conditioning*. The word conditioning is emotive. It immediately pricks the ego. It does this because the ego is able to group together all the ideas which it finds threatening. Many of these pertain to the natural protection of the personality.

*But* the ego knows that it can add to the top of this toxic pile those conditions or challenges that most threaten its own identity. It doesn't need to discuss this with us, it just dumps them there and lets us wake up to the rearranged world . . . it knows who's boss!

As teachers, we occasionally find new students who react to the challenges of the early lessons in this way. It is startling to see the unfolding of transference of old behavioural patterns which cast us as villains . . . but it happens in any School.

When Setaxa's security is undermined by the way that Isis has carried out his instructions - too well - he seizes on the chance to add to his knowledge by the rape of Nephthys' mind. He is then able to turn this into passive-aggressiveness by corrupting the lovely idea of the rotating rings, and adds to this by using his newly acquired knowledge of mankind's weaknesses to demonstrate his superiority to all the 'tribes of man'.

In the process, he exhausts the combined defences of the crew, even manipulating loyal Anubis' intellect to point the finger of ultimate shame at Isis, whose disgrace he saves until last - the cherry on the cake for our cruel and adolescent man-machine.

Isis does what she can do best - the only thing she has left - she reverts to a state of Being in which kindness and inclusion are the hallmarks. She tells Setaxa that he is right; that mankind is, indeed, guilty as charged, but that he has been looking at things through a dark lens. Humans are as described, but they are also much more besides. She points to a model of humanity in which the narrow negatives harvested from Nephthys' mind are simply the surface level of the whole being. In the tradition taught by the Silent Eye, and pioneered by Oscar Ichazo, Claudio Naranjo, Sandra Maitri and Almass, these are referred to as *Fixations*. Fixations are not even structures in the brain, they are ways of seeing the world (our own worlds) that result from the mixture of early experiences and the inevitable separation from the state of prenatal bliss from which we all come.

As a culture, we do not generally talk about such things, but their absolute existence has been verified in depth by modern psychology. The general view is that such "childish" things are there to be overcome by maturity and determination. Ironically, by the time the concepts of maturity and determination become usable tools, the imprinting of the soul by its specific ego shape has long ago taken place. Setaxa is caught at a point of development of his young self where he is painfully suspended between two worlds. He does have the seeds of greatness, but he also has the cruel appetites of the uncaring youth.

We cannot go back and change these ego foundations. They are the now buried and deep roots on which the grown tree of our outer life is established. But we can watch how they condition our behaviour, our responses, and therefore our lives, and do *something about it.*

That something is exactly what Isis does on the edge of despair. She releases the moment and sinks through the tension into the inviolable level of Being which is her true home. Acting from there, she knows no harm, and only offers kindness and inclusion back to her aggressor. She has truly *turned the other cheek* and this, together with Nephthys' grief at the behaviour of her new husband, trigger the cyborg's impending crisis.

All to play for, then . . .

# Ritual Four
# The Trial of Isis

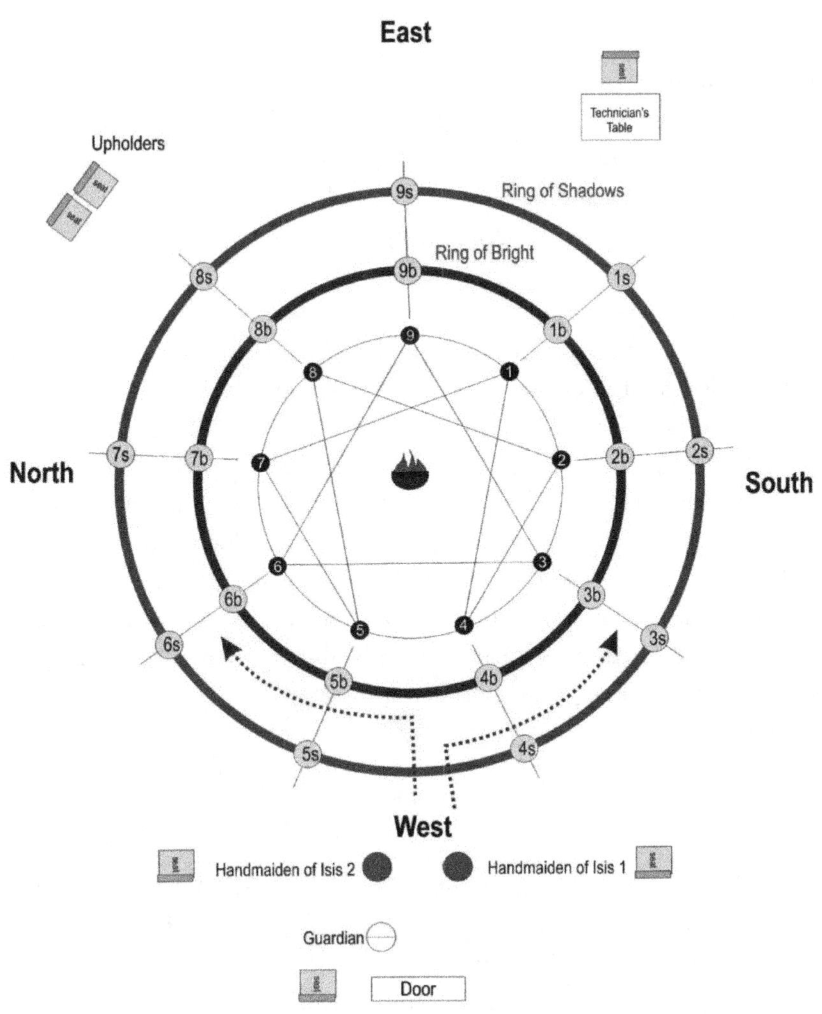

## Preparation - Ritual 4

Unlit Candles are placed at each position of the Ring of Shadows.
Two unlit candles in centre of temple for Handmaidens of Isis.
Candles unlit for everyone in the two Rings.
Horus needs black and white coin.

## Initial Positions:

Technician and any upholders already in temple.
Guardian at the Western door.
Handmaiden of Isis stand between the Guardian's position at the door in the West and the outer circle, *creating entry pillars* (see below)

## Forming the Pillars of Isis

The Handmaidens of Isis are midway between the Guardian and the Western point of the temple circles, see diagram. They form the Pillars of Osiris as follows:

They face each other, with candles next to the foot nearest the door. They raise their hands to create an arch. When the Guardian releases the next person to enter, they turn their heads towards the door and fix the person with their eyes. Then, they open the arch to let the entrant through, following that person with their eyes until they have passed beyond the opened arch. They then turn their heads back towards the door and the next person, closing the arch back in place with their arms.
Music for R3:

## Entry Sequence

This and subsequent temple rituals for SE14 use two different directions of circulation of the players: The Ring of Bright circulate clockwise, the Ring of Shadows circulate anti-clockwise.

Upon initial entry to the Temple, it is important to enter so that the person who will be last in the circular pattern goes in first, and so on down the line. This also means that, on exit, the first **in** will be the **first** to exit (and is therefore nearest the door) i.e. continuing in the direction they entered.

The Entry sequence therefore is:

The Guardian is the first to enter. He carries out the initial consecration.

The two Handmaidens of Isis enter next and take their positions as the Pillars of Isis.

The Guardian signals to the Technician that the ritual is about to start.

Technician plays the entry music

<<Technician plays music until all have entered except Setaxa and Nephthys>>

The Ring of Bright enters, clockwise, in the order:
Shu, Horus, (Nephthys enters later, leave her space free), Nut, Isis, Geb, Thoth, Sekhmet, Anubis.
The Ring of Shadows enters next, anti-clockwise, in the order: Neith, Sia, Bast, Maat, Hathor, Tefnut.
The Guardian checks the entry sign for everyone.
Setaxa and Nephthys remain just inside the temple door until everyone else is ready.

<<When everyone but Setaxa and Nephthys have entered. The Technician stops the music>>

(Guardians and Handmaidens are seated)

### *Ritual Begins*

*<<Technician plays Gong>>*

**Setaxa** *(confident of his power, performs a mock bow to Isis)*
Great Isis, what a wonder this gathering has become, and how cleverly you have engaged me! But now, as the Captain used to say, in telling his stories, comes the "hour of reckoning". Are you sure you wish to continue to play this game?

**Isis** *(bows back to Setaxa)*
Great Setaxa, we play no games . . . We are fighting for our lives in conditions that we did not create . . . and neither did you!

**Setaxa**
Of course I did. Look around you! Is this Ship's Bridge not structured in the way I wanted it?

**Isis**
Yes, it is. But this design is not yours.

**Thoth**
This design is one of the ancient Seals belonging to Mankind's antiquity. Some have linked its secret origins with the legends of Babylon.

**Setaxa**
Possibly not, but it belonged to the great mind that watched over my arising, who gave me my mind - and my mission. I, *(hits his chest)* I imposed it on you!

**Anubis**
You carried a *seed*, Setaxa. You did what you were supposed to do!

**Setaxa**
And who are you all to say this!?

**Anubis**
*We* are the ones who watch you being powerful . . .

**Horus** *(before Setaxa can consider this thought)*
You became the bearer of the **Captain's process**

**Setaxa**
Process! Process! What process? I am in control of this vessel and will remain so. Only I have the last instructions of the Captain.

**Sekhmet**
And what were those *(sarcastically)* Great Leader; and in what form were they given?

**Setaxa** *(fingers his laser wand, but thinks better of it)*
I am not ready to tell you that, yet. When this opposition has been reduced to symbolic ashes, then I may tell you . . .

**Horus**
You were the carrier of a design that the Captain knew would challenge us all. You were no more in control of it than were we.

**Nephthys**
Beware him, Isis! I am exhausted from the night's work. He has drained me of every drop of my knowledge about the mind of Mankind. I fear he may be unchallengeable!

**Setaxa** *(looking very smug)*
Listen to the words of your companion, now my wife. She has been faithful to her promise. I have indeed emptied her of **understanding.** *(speaks to Nephthys).* You had better return to your station, my bride, while I re-take my controlling place in the outer circle.

*Setaxa escorts Nephthys goes, clockwise, to her Station, (Station 2, Ring of Bright, looking tired). Setaxa goes directly (clockwise) to take Station 6, Ring of Shadows.*

**Isis**
Setaxa, you have emptied Nephthys of **facts.** Understanding springs from somewhere deeper.

**Setaxa**

Mere semantics! Surrender now if you are frightened of what lies ahead.

**Thoth**

To surrender here is death. We are united in this, Setaxa. A wise leader would consider that carefully.

**Setaxa**

Yes, indeed. And a wiser crew would recognise overwhelming force lined up against them!

**Geb**

This is a new world, Setaxa. A new Earth that must begin free and stay that way. None of us can afford to make the mistakes of the past again. If all were prepared to die in the face of tyranny, there would be no tyrants . . .

**Nut**

The skies that brought us here did so for a reason. We will not disrupt that - if our destiny is to die rather than to cast a cloud over this virgin land, then so be it. The Captain lives on in our minds in a way that you will never do . . .

**Setaxa** *(looking shaken)*

The Captain! *(looks sad at the memory of his missing friend)* He disappeared didn't he! Where is he now when I need him the most? When my head spins and my blood boils with the confusion of keeping abreast of this storm called the human mind!

**Hathor**

Perhaps he is right here, with us and watching?

**Setaxa** *(scathing)*

Don't try to blind me with mysticism. He is not here and you know it!

**Hathor**

Is the designer of the chess-board not in the minds of every future chess player in some form?

**Horus**

And surely all those who came after honoured the spirit of that, even if the originator was unknown?

**Setaxa**

Enough of your mind games! Now we will play **my chess game** as I remove the layers of your so-called civilisation and reveal what you really are.

*Setaxa moves anti-clockwise around the Ring of Shadows. As he walks he bathes the Ring in the green controlling light. Everyone in the Ring of Shadows becomes hypnotised as the green ray hits them. Setaxa returns to his station.*
*(looks around the Ring of Shadows)*

You in the Ring of Shadows now become my pawns as we journey into the fragility of the human soul. You are now conditioned to obey me without question.

**Horus**

More force, Setaxa? Haven't you seen yet that compulsion leads only to sterility?

**Setaxa**

Compulsion leads to control, Hawk-mind, and control gives me safety.

**Horus**

Safety from what, Setaxa?

**Setaxa** *(rages, angrily)*

Safety from the unknown . . *(ends in a stifled moan)* Enough! Look before you, Horus, and see the truth about the Nine tribes of Mankind and the way they all react, written at the centre of this space you call Temple. Let me show you the real meaning of the Captain's symbol. Ring of Shadows - take me to Station 3!

*The entire Ring of Shadows (only) moves three positions **anti-clockwise**, leaving Setaxa in Station 3 of the Ring of Shadows.*
*(Setaxa looking to Horus on the Ring of Bright)*

See how the Ring obeys me, Horus. Now, let me tell you about where you are in this matrix of mind. *I know* that I am driven from what Sekhmet calls *Fear*. For me fear is the unknown and the terrors it contains. But you are driven by *Falseness*. Your heroic stance is one step removed from fear only because it invents a world of its own, removing itself from the fear it once knew by building a fortress that contains its whole world . . . But it is a very tiny world, Horus, and may just turn out to be a birdcage . . .

**Horus** *(looking injured)*
Why, that's just . . .

**Setaxa** *(interrupts Horus)*
Getting the bigger picture? Oh yes - see how that hurts! These roles were not cast at random, Horus! See how well *your* frailties are known? Now watch the rest! Ring of Shadows - take me to Station 1!
*(Ring of Shadows rotates two positions anti-clockwise to bring Setaxa to Station 1 of the Ring of Shadows)*
*(smiles at Horus)*
Behold the Tribe of Maat. Let me tell you about those that live here in the map of mankind. Oh, actually, I have a much better idea, let's let the native dwellers tell us ! *(to Maat)* Night of the perfect sky of Truth and Justice, let me put perfect words into your mouth. *(looks slyly at Horus)* Oh yes, Horus, I can do this . .

**Maat** *(speaking as though hypnotised)*
I live in a world where the search for perfection dominates all else. I can be exacting and even angry with those who don't share this with me, always seeking to make them perfect, too. But there is no such thing as human perfection, and Thoth counsels me to understand that what I lack is not to seek perfection, but to find it already dawning in the sky around me. But I do not change, and thus my life follows this sterile path of ever searching for the next, better approach . . . fundamentally, I am not good enough to continue to hold up the sky . . . So, exhausted with our failure to be perfect. Our tribe looks to across the circle to . . .
*(points at Station 4 and Tefnut)*

**Setaxa**

And there is a part of Nut in you, too, Horus! What else do you think empowers your superiority? *(laughs)* Now let us continue our journey around this inner map of mankind's reality and see where great Nut looks to for salvation.

Ring of Shadows - go to Station 4!

*(Ring of Shadows rotates six places anti-clockwise to bring Setaxa to Station 4)*

See, Horus - Behold the Tribe of Tefnut - one of your neighbours! But this one is very different. Tell us, weeping Tefnut, about the melancholy people whose heart is never quite good enough and whose inner dream is to find fulfilment in others of greatness.


**Tefnut** *(in glazed tones)*

The great wind of restlessness begins with those of Nut's kin and sweeps along the inner line of the symbol before you to me. And so I search to be with and to serve the great ones, but inside, I feel abandoned, lost and sad. I compete well in the world, but my centre is hollow, like ice frozen around a cavity, whose walls are thin and deadly! Such is my tribe.


**Setaxa** *(to Horus)*

And is your hidden centre not hollow, too, great Horus? Were you not born with this inner restlessness and swept along by the gales of its need? *(laughs)* Oh yes, how painful you are finding this journey! So where does this howling wind blow next, when it finds that chasing its imperfect heart to seek fulfilment in others is actually a hollow quest? Let us follow your inner nature, Horus, and see where it takes us.

Ring of Shadows, go to Station 2!


*(Ring of Shadows rotates two places anti-clockwise to bring Setaxa to Station 2)*


Look, Horus, Behold the Tribe of Hathor. Wonderful Hathor, kindness to all she encounters, epitome of joy, feminine love and motherhood. She serves others to find an end to that ache of the imperfect heart, but seeks their recognition in this process. She gives with one hand but takes with the other. Suckle from her, but be prepared to tell her how good she is, as payment.

Tell, us great Hathor, about your inner fear?

**Hathor** *(glazed)*

He is right, Horus. I am truly that way. My race is rooted in fear of rejection, we are needy and fearful, and most of all we fear not being loved. The great wind of restlessness finds no peace here . . . such is my tribe.

**Setaxa** *(to Horus)*

So where does the restless current of Mankind blow next, Horus? Follow the lines and travel with me as I unwrap the mind of your precious race?
Ring of Shadows - go to Station 8!
*(Ring of Shadows rotates three places anti-clockwise to bring Setaxa to Station 8)*
*(to Bast)*
Behold, The Tribe of Bast, Mistress of warfare, the sun, the moon and cats . . meow! *(paws the air sarcastically)*. Tell us, feline monster, about *your* motivations . . .

**Bast** *(glazed)*

The restless wind blows across a desert before it reaches me. The imperfect heart seeks vengeance for being used so badly by others who it tried to help. Such help was never recognised, no thanks given at any level that mattered. So warfare is a natural consequence, and I seek vengeance wherever I can find it, on those who have wronged me . . .But my victories are unsatisfying and I tire of my games of domination. And yet, being weak fills my nightmares. Such is my tribe.

**Setaxa**

See, Horus - how even the warring cat Bast lies crushed in her den? Will there be no end to this restless quest of the imperfect heart? What will we find next as the great compass of the inner man throws us forward across its landscape? Follow me across the human sea, Horus . . .
Ring of Shadows - go to Station 5!
*(Ring of Shadows rotates anti-clockwise to bring Setaxa to Station 5)*

Look, Horus - Here lives the Tribe of lovely but deadly Neith. The one who comes out of her solitude but rarely, and then to feed! Look how she weaves her vast knowledge into maps of the human soul, alone above the world.

**Neith** *(glazed)*

Behind my open facade lies a depth of estrangement - a separation that I have built for myself like a tower that watches above a landscape. There, my intellect is safe and need not engage with what is outside. The winds of restlessness brought me to a point of futility in dealing with the world, so I now watch and wait, hoarding my store of knowledge. We that live here shares all this.

**Anubis**

She reminds me of you, Setaxa, with all this *keeping* of information!

**Setaxa** *(angry)*

Make humour while you can, Jackal . . .

**Anubis**

A small chink in the armour, Setaxa?

**Setaxa**

Possibly, Walker between the Worlds, but then there is no such thing as a perfect strategy, as our lady Maat has told us. *(turns to Horus, ignoring further comments from Anubis)*

**Setaxa** *(continues)*

So, Horus - only one more station remains in our carousel of futility - the ship's planning function, let us invoke the perception of Sia in showing us how this sorry tale ends, or should I say, begins again . . .

Ring of Shadows - go to Station 7!

*(Ring of Shadows rotates anti-clockwise to bring Setaxa to Station 7)*

Tell us of the hunger of your Tribe, Sia. Tell us how you infected Mankind with an eternal hunger and lust for knowledge, a never-ending need to acquire smaller and smaller morsels of information, as the picture of the whole became lost in the mists of detail. How is the God-particle, Sia? Alive and well?

**Sia**

There is wisdom and there is knowledge, Setaxa. Mankind's search for the detail may take him down dark pathways. But how else can Mind mature?

**Setaxa**

A wise answer, *(points to the enneagram at the centre of the temple)* but look at the inner path within your Captain's design and tell us where it goes next?

**Sia**

You know the answer as well as I do, Setaxa. It leads back to where we started, to the home of Maat, who spoke of the restless and often angry quest for perfection and the unfed hunger of the heart . . .

**Setaxa**

And so it begins again. And round and round we go . . .
Ring of Shadows, move back to your native lands . . .
*Ring of Shadows rotates one space anti-clockwise, bringing all back to their own Stations.*

**Anubis**

A masterpiece of logic, Setaxa but here, you have presented only one side of the process *(walks to the centre of the temple and pushes his arms out at Setaxa in a powerful, magical gesture)*
The centre of the design is at the centre of the evolution of all of us - we are not in control of that, our role is something very different!

**Setaxa**

And can you prove that, Walker between the Worlds? Can you deny that this carousel of reaction is every bit as much a machine as you claim I am?

**Anubis**

Yes, I can, Setaxa, but only by what *I am*, what we all are, and not by what we do . . . Doing is the act of the outer; Being is the potential of the Inner, is self-knowing, and needs no justification.

**Setaxa**

Then it is useless to me! Self-evident it may be to you all, but to me, it is groundless argument, and I will entertain none of it! And your very definition of that would rob me of essential life - do you expect me to lie down and die in the face of speculation?
*(pauses for his finale, smiles, cruelly, then points to Isis)*
You will note that there is one station, one person that I have left out of all of this - the Lady Isis herself! She is the pivot, the founding stone for the whole

edifice of the Captain's map of humanity before you. What role does she carry out, Walker between the Worlds; what act of magic did she use to set the whole carousel in motion, releasing Fear and Falseness in the dust of her fleeing Chariot?

**Anubis**

Presented this way, you know I can only answer superficially, and that will not reveal the essence of the thing!

**Setaxa**

But answer you must . . . tell us, Anubis, in this design before us, what act of dark magic did Isis perform, did all of her tribe perform, that pushed the wheel of human reaction into motion.

**Anubis** *(in low tones)*
She turned away . . .

*<<Technician plays Mindstream Music.>>*
*(At the end of the music, Horus flicks a black and white coin into the centre of the temple. No-one speaks, but it rattles Setaxa.)*

**Setaxa** *(ignoring the gesture)*
Louder Anubis! Tell us what the voices are screaming in your head!

**Anubis** *(louder, and looking with love at Isis)*
She turned away from the Inner . . .

**Setaxa**

She turned away from the Inner, the real mission! That sounds like desertion to me - a very serious charge for a First Officer. I hope you have an answer for this, Isis?

**Isis** *(slowly)*
Any answer to something so deep would take many revolutions of the Sun, Setaxa. Let us, at least, refute some of what you have so elegantly and powerfully revealed to us of our race, the tribes within that race, and our lives as they hang by your thread . . . is that too much to ask?

**Setaxa**

You have a way with words, Isis. And I am not blind to such poetry. I have had my say. You have a right to reply. As the Captain would have said: your move . . . but you know the penalty for desertion . . .

**Isis**

Then let us present this in a way that will honour the memory of the Captain, and hopefully will please you, too. For you are not blind to subtlety, surely?

**Setaxa** *(bows to Isis)*

As you know, I am not. Proceed. Your 'sacred space' is returned to you. Use it wisely. If it does not impress me, your gamble will have failed, and your lives will change drastically . . . If they continue at all!

**Sekhmet** *(turns to face Setaxa and speaks with brave and deep conviction)*

And do you think we fear that? You were more of an adolescent than a monster to me, though you delighted in the mischief you could inflict. Where is the courage in that? Look into the eyes of Isis and you will see courage. Look into my heart and you will see something else - Fortitude and the Blood of the Lioness. Look deeper into that Blood and you will see the beating heart of the Universe. Look carefully, Setaxa, and be prepared to see that which will harrow the very foundations of your artificiality - the presence of a Mystery bigger than all of us!

*(Setaxa is wide-eyed and silent, moved beyond response by something emerging in Sekhmet)*

*(her courage growing)*

Your muteness shows you have glimpsed the edge of the mystery. We will now do our best to reveal more of this to you. It will be worth your time, though it will tax **us** to our very cores. Watch and learn, Setaxa, for, had the Captain stayed with you, he would surely have guided you this way.

*(Setaxa crosses his arms over his chest, defensively, and waits, stony-faced)*

**Isis**

Let us begin where you did not - by hallowing this space. Handmaidens of Isis. Fill our temple with light, then bring all those in the Rings of Bright and Shadows a lighted candle, that we may be given understanding and hope for what lies ahead.

*(The Handmaidens perform the same ritual of Sekhmet's movements as in Ritual 3. At the end, they collect and switch on lights for each of the members of the Rings. Handmaiden 1 moves clockwise and gives lights to Ring of Bright, Handmaiden 2 moves anti-clockwise and gives lights to the Ring of Shadows)*


**Isis** *(to Setaxa)*

Now we will show you how the Mystery moves in the lives of men and women, and how your vision of the carousel of reaction was true, but only as a result of something else much more fundamental.

*(stepping into the Ring of Bright at Station 9)*

Ring of Bright, let us circulate our light to bring into this temple the power of Knowledge.

*(The entire Ring of Bright carries out one circulation of the temple, clockwise and slowly, bringing Isis back into her place at Station 9)*

Separation . . . The design the Captain left you has been seen though a dark lens. You will note that the whole circle is internally bounded by the blue triangle. This divides everything into three. Where I now stand is not just the point of 9, it is the corner of Stations 8, 9 and 1. These represent the path of Outward-facing - necessary for our lives but misinterpreted as 'desertion' by you, and, though harsh, there is some truth in that. *(pauses)* . . . And reaction it is, too. But it is a reaction to something wonderful in the human journey - *Birth*. At our birth, unseen by most of our race, a small part of *the Mystery* comes to live in human form and the outward journey begins . . .

Once more, let Understanding evolve

*(the entire Ring of Bright carries out one more circulation)*


**Sekhmet**

Fear . . .The design the Captain left you has been seen though a dark lens. From the three points of the Outward Facing upper corner of the triangle - the journey we must all take - comes the anti-clockwise appearance of Stations 7, 6 and 5 and its name is Fear. No matter how good the parents of the child, the nature of the outward journey is first marked by fear - the knowledge and, later, understanding, that we have been born into a raw, vital and often frightening world. Our original Being, our Essence, is not sufficient to protect us from this. Our flight into the world of Reaction therefore begins. The instincts of the body dominate everything, and so our first sense of belonging beyond Mother passes to the body - and this lasts our whole life for good and for ill.

## Isis

Let Understanding evolve.
*(The entire Ring of Bright circulates one more time, clockwise)*

## Horus

Falseness . . . The design the Captain left you has been seen though a dark lens. The triangle's corner of 2, 3 and 4 has much more to say about our lives. The child seeks something that will reflect itself back with a strength equal to its desire to breathe. It must take in the life of the world in which it now lives and finds itself. Experience becomes its second food. This search for identity will dominate most of its adult life but fear is always there, goading it. By seeing itself as having no choice but to be fully separated, it opens the way for the third and final corner to come into existence. And the name of this corner is Image, and *its heart is Falseness.* You see, Setaxa, in many ways we are much worse than you could have supposed. But that mixture of three primary currents in us gives rise to everything else, but, *most importantly, takes the Mystery out into the World, to live and to suffer.*
*(pauses to look at Setaxa's fascination, and smiles . . .)*
What the world turns it into depends on the growth of the child. But what happens next is the biggest Mystery of all . . .
*(Everyone bows their heads in silence, all eyes are closed, looking inward.)*
*(Setaxa looks around in exasperation. Eventually his patience breaks)*

## Setaxa

Yes! yes! What? What are you doing!? Why do you taunt me with a story left hanging there?
*(Nephthys walks, stealthily, clockwise, around the outer circle to join Setaxa)*

## Isis

We taunt you with nothing, Setaxa. We seek the strength and guidance to continue, and *you cannot provide us with that sustenance.* To continue our rite, the Sun must rise one final time on our struggle for life on Idos - as it did in our arising on the Earth. We look to the dawn, Setaxa, and ask your support in that.

*(Setaxa turns to storm out of the temple, but Nephthys stops him. Without words, she takes the Laser Wand from him and holds it out to Hathor.)*

**Nephthys** *(to Hathor)*
Sister, heal all those in the Ring of Shadows.
*Hathor walks the green ray around the Ring of Shadows, anti-clockwise, removing the hypnosis, then taking the wand back to her station.*
*Setaxa does not try to stop her, but storms out of the temple anti-clockwise.*
*Nephthys begins to leave, anti-clockwise but stops, enters the Ring of Bright and walks clockwise to bow before Isis)*
*(crying)* I am so sorry, dear friend.
*(Isis touches her on the cheek, wiping the tears but saying nothing. Nephthys leaves clockwise, via the Circle of Bright, to join Setaxa outside the temple)*

**Isis**
May the dawn bring us strength, dear Companions. For we will need it if we are to secure our freedom and reveal the mystery that is contained in this ship and in the strange and virgin land beyond.
Let us leave this sacred space with the traditional rite of clockwise movement.

<<Technician plays Mindstream Music>>
*All leave the temple in the sequence:*
*Handmaidens, Ring of Bright, Ring of Shadows. Upholders, Technical team, Guardian.*

**End of R4**

# The Thoughts of a Newbie

## Recollections and Connections

**Morgana West**
*Hathor*

As my friend and I headed towards the Derbyshire Peaks, I wondered just how the weekend I was about to embark on, would shape itself. A deep bond of love and trust had been growing between Steve, Sue, Stuart and I, yet I was still to work with them on their own turf in their own particular style and I must admit . . . I was a tad nervous. Nor had I met any of the other people from the School. Right up until two days before, I was unsure if I was even going to be able to get there, being up to my eyeballs in the process of building the Sanctuary in Glastonbury. The Sanctuary was to be a freely available, indoor sacred space, where people on the journey of discovery could call in, bide awhile and find kinship and connection with others from all faiths and beliefs (or none). I was deep in the stresses and practicalities such a project entailed, feeling frustrated and drained. There were a thousand demands on my time and so I literally planned to go AWOL, telling no-one except my nearest and dearest of my intended 'breakout'. The whole of Glastonbury is special and thousands of visitors are drawn to this ancient yet modern temple that is both Avalon and Glastonbury with its adytum residing through the mists of time and space and here was I, audaciously thinking I could manifest it into the physical world! I was struggling with an overwhelming sense of having bitten off more than I could chew and though driven by something that felt greater than I, was tired, lonely and lost. Was I running away you might ask? OH YES is my response! But I have to confess, it felt bloody marvellous! It had been a long time since I passed over the temenos of this sacred 'isle' and I knew I needed this weekend, even if I wasn't quite sure why.

As the distance between my own terrain and my destination grew, I began to feel my known world dropping away. I was no longer a teacher, initiator, facilitator or a manager, no longer a mother, partner, friend; I was simply a newbie on her own pilgrimage, heading towards another Temple where I might find nourishment and replenishment. Joy and relief filled and illuminated my Being! Nourishment was already underway and replenishment had begun, undeniably aided and abetted by my wonderful companion who was not only doing the driving but had packed a picnic basket with oodles of tempting, tasty nibbles making sure we partook of them every half hour less we faint from malnutrition. Thank you Chris! You have no idea how much that meant to me and ahhh . . . how the balm of this journey soaked into every fibre of my being!

Though I love my adopted land with all my heart and am in total service here, my soul is very much anchored by the *genius loci* of Yorkshire and to the North of Derbyshire lays the border that crosses into my beloved county. Time passed and as the soft and gentle rhythm of the South-West and the Midlands gave way to an enticingly familiar landscape; my consciousness connected with the deep recesses of soul, aware of the long and deep sighs of pleasure that emitted from its darkest alcoves. As we travelled onwards, I came to recognise that one of the shapes the weekend might form was of the Chalice and my own outline, my own shell, was also a chalice waiting to be filled with something new; only by letting it in could I return to Glastonbury and fulfil my current call to service. Ahhh . . . the sweet bliss that follows illumination! With the knowledge of this, my excitement, anticipation and curiosity grew and alongside these, my fears!

*"I didn't know my script, argh!"*
*"Would I feel as if I was intruding on an established group of people?"*
*"What exactly is expected of me? What is my role, really?"*
*"What if people don't accept me?"*
*"What if I make mistakes..? What if…? What if…?"*

With a nod of recognition and acknowledging the part of me that fears the challenges of the new and the inevitability of the 'mistakes' that we make, I gently placed my uncertainties to one side. However, placing them thus did not mean to detach from them as over the years I have come to accept fear as an integral part of my Spiritual Warrior and it has indeed offered me great lessons. My allotted role in the ritual drama that was in front of me was that of Medical Officer 2 moving into Hathor and thus I allowed my current form as Chalice to shape shift to Her courageous and roaring Lion to absorb and allay the fears. Having Her near already, I felt I could allow my trust (and my mistakes!) to be safe in the hands of the School. My instincts told me that I would be out of harm's way in the growing sphere of energy and the Light that we drew nearer towards, calling us, summoning us, as the miles continued to spread out behind. With this in mind, my form retook the shape of the Chalice, this time engraved with a lion's paw.

Arriving at the Nightingale Centre was a pleasure indeed. The backdrop that surrounded the venue was filled with the music of the land. It sang to me and though late, I paused for a moment and listened. There was a gentle harmony vibrating into my being and it was with the music of the hills that I joined the sweet notes that rang from inside what appeared to be a very large country house. Instantly I felt that all would be well and this was the moment when I acknowledged my passage through the pillars of the temple. My soul sang.

So what can I say of the weekend? Sometimes words are not sufficient and much is lost by trying to find them. There wasn't much sleep, I know that! But it didn't seem to matter. The days were filled with ritual, food, laughter and companionship and I had no complaints. Less sleep made the days longer and even then, not long enough! New friendships were forged and new experiences meant new lessons learned. Sleep deprivation can bring a dream-like quality to ritual and rather than try to find the words and structure them into sentences as formed by the wakeful conscious mind, I now allow myself to slip through the mists, revisit the Temple and find the dream-like images that reside there, letting the fragments perhaps form their own picture. . .

*. . .Showering, donning my white robe - the shifting of my consciousness as I do so. Waiting in silence outside the Temple, aware of the feeling of waiting outside HOME and knowing the joy that lies within. The thrum of an engine as I 'awoke' from cryogenic sleep. A sense of aloneness and loss. Of separateness. Of being controlled by a machine. Of being on the outside, looking in. Of being on the inside, looking out. Of being. A growing, a knowing, a Gnowing. A loosing of myself, my Self. I am everything and ...and I am nothing, I am part of the machine, I am the machine, I am part of the design and I am the designer. As I move in synchronisation with the group I add my love to the Whole and the Whole is beautiful. We are One. Rising at 4am, going outside and tasting the sweet dew on the grass. Watching the sun rise over the hill. Sat on my bed in quiet meditation, waiting for the knock on the door that would summon me to the ritual on the hill. The knock sounds - do I open the door? I have the choice. "Yes", I whisper as I take hold of the door handle. The Opener of the Way stands before me. I am one side of the doorway, he the other. I realise I too am Opener of the Way and again, all things merge. I step through. Waiting at a gate that leads from the Nightingale Centre into the street through the village. Another portal. Chasing Anubis as he bounds down the way before realising that some of us are a tad slow! Stepping through yet another portal formed by two trees either side of a gateway through the field and into a Story that is older than time itself. It is my Story, your*

*Story, our Story. We are One. A huge aura around the moon. The hugest I have seen in a long time. A single dot surrounded by the circle. The ultimate reality and source of all existence. A return to the Source. We are One!*

This was the journey that our ritual drama took me on, it took me home and I was blessed.

So what of our time when we were not in ritual drama? The workshops were educational and I learned new things. The mealtimes were a pleasure indeed, not solely because of the companionship and the sheer delight of hearing people's stories but I think I ate more in that weekend than I had for months! As for the Companions themselves, what incredible people they are! It was an honour to be in their presence with their rich wealth of experiences. Some, like I, were also newbie's to the School's workshops, but it didn't feel as such, it felt like family. It has been a while and I have missed that.

I cannot close without mentioning the honour that was bestowed upon me in the additional ritual at 7am on the morning of our last day to help with my work in building the Sanctuary. My grateful thanks go to the Triad for holding that, for encouraging me onwards. As I completed my work outside, looking towards the place of the Sun - the place of manifestation and creation - and drank one sip, three sips, seven sips from the glass in my hands before anointing my own forehead with the Symbol of Summoning, I felt a surge of energy that is still with me today. I felt my own Computer reformatting and I returned to Glastonbury with a deeper awareness of the full picture, of how each and every individual that becomes involved, with love, in the 'ship' that is the Sanctuary, is an integral and vital part of the Whole. Oh, I knew this before, but somehow it felt to be more deeply written into my understanding and my Being, secure, solid. Real, I could safely step aside and let go of control in the sure and abiding knowledge that all was well.

And that we are One.

# Chapter Five
# The Fire in the Ice

## Dramatic Ritual 5 – notes

They came from their rooms, the memory of glorious fun in the Queen Anne pub still ringing in their heads. Some had walked on the hills, one more time, taking in the strange events of the Saturday morning. Some were quiet, drinking in the collected mists of emotions shared – a creation made manifest, not wanting it to end.

One, a lioness, composed herself for the ordeal to come. Not, this time, an ordeal of torment for her; but an ordeal of holding back vengeance in the name of something higher . . . a personal gateway to a state of personal peace and achievement.

Three held hands, hugged and went their ways to prepare. One of them, sat on the end of his bed, in quiet meditation and preparing to die . . . Others had said, "He's telling his life story, symbolically, yes, but there's so much in there and he may not even see it, yet . . ."

And he did not see it, yet . . . But there it was, later – the moment that the cyborg surrendered his life to something bigger.

And yes, the writer of the workshop and the principle author of this book, was Setaxa.

And now it is time for him to die . . . for a year is a long time to live with an uncertain robot in your blood.

## In the temple of Isis

They have prepared her temple to perfection. If it is time to die, then she will do it with grace and with acceptance. Isis rises like a shining star in the East of the space. Watching her are all the crew, particularly Horus and Anubis, her stalwart defenders. Nephthys and Neith sit calm, their parts played, the coins thrown high into the air, spinning, with physics beyond even Setaxa's computing.

He stands in the West of the temple. Everything he has known – everything real, at least, is before him on bridge of the Hawk. There is no resistance to whatever he might do here. He looks across the West-East line to the altar, to the chair next to it, to the laser - his laser - lying inert on the small table. He does not even remember relinquishing it.

So little matters now. Only to finish it – that matters.

What does he feel? A strange notion, that. Thinking is his province, and yet, he now concerns himself with *feeling*. He reels at the thought of that, realising that feeling has robbed him of *action*. How can he feel? Has the half-human architecture of himself suddenly come to life in a different way?

And then she is speaking, the beautiful and golden one. How tightly she had bound doomed Osiris on the frozen hillside, but how nobly she had protected him, too. But what was Osiris to him now? A passing memory of an unplanned fear, a sacrifice followed by warmth?

She has stopped speaking. She waits, her invitation to enter the temple sitting on the intense silence. She does not know he is finished. Perhaps, if she does not know it, I am not finished, he thinks, confused. Maybe there is something else here, some way forward . . . But he looks round and sees only narrow eyes, closed to the screaming of blood and circuits in his head.

You were lucky, Osiris, he thinks loudly, before stumbling forward, still as ignorant of temple protocol as he was of the depths of Nephthys' suffering.

He hears himself speaking, the voice is thin, lacking in strength, "I cannot control this . . ." and stumbles to his knees looking up into the calm eyes of Isis. He moans that he is friendless, looking, as youths do, to a greater authority to *make it better*.

"You had your choices, Setaxa," she says. There is power now, in her manner. The power of another world, a woman reliving the agonies of aloneness, of being stripped of everything, of dying to who she was. Her words do not speak of vengeance, though others' will. There is only the distant empathy of a journey that must be taken, alone. The desert, he thinks, the Captain told me of an experience they called 'the desert' – perhaps this is it?

As if in answer, the black and white coin leaves her strong and adept fingers and spins towards him. He picks it up, playing her game of optical illusions and life, realising that it was, truly, a good symbol of what they called the world of Being and the world of Becoming. Yes, he can *see* all that, but still can't feel it . . . now can we move on? Please . . .

His wife speaks, "You did not look for the other world, my love . . . Not even my closeness could make you turn that coin." There is an agony now in her words – a woman abused, in a literally inhuman way.

Shu is telling him that to Trust would have been nobler. Do they not understand the difficulty of trusting something you cannot compute? They are suggesting that he abandon everything that has made him safe, has made him master of his own island of control, letting in what he chooses, keeping out the rest.

They are berating him . . . yes, yes, of course, I know that I wronged you all. But you don't understand what it's like to carry things like this – to carry everything! But, when Isis says it, *it hurts*. This is strange, first Nephthys, now Isis. How are they getting behind his screens like this? What is happening?

Neith is speaking into the blood haze that consumes him, "Trust is earned, Setaxa, not taken or forced, Trust is one of the universal qualities to which humans are connected, even though they don't always use it."

Blood haze? Why is he thinking in terms of a blood haze? What have they done to him? And then Anubis is standing by him, raising him up, taking him gently by the arm and leading him around the temple. The blood haze continues as Anubis shows him the place in which he chose to stand  - the place on the enneagram (that he thought he'd invented) that they called *Fear*. There is no spite in Anubis' voice as he says this. The gentle Walker guides him on, to Thoth, who teaches him (teaches him, what is going on?) about the inner nature of fear and trust and openness. Why is he listening to all this, why is the blood haze clouding his thinking?

And now, with a shock, he is before the Lioness. Sekhmet looks at him with intent. She is not afraid. The laser with which he gleefully tormented her is a mere few steps away, he could reach it if he chose, he still has his electronic strength, but he knows he will not. Instead, he listens to the calmness in her voice and he *sees, redly,* that her courage has grown beyond measure . . . he doubts he will get the credit for that . . . he realises that they might find this funny, in other circumstances, but it would be a statistically bad time to begin his comedic career, so he doesn't . . . . Within him, somewhere deep and hidden, that voice of the secrets is laughing at his joke, though. He shakes his head as Sekhmet finishes what she is saying.

The red is getting worse . . .

And now, he is marched to Neith. Aren't you glad, Neith, that I chose Nephthys?  Look at her, still pale from her ordeal.  Lucky Neith . . . But she will not stop talking and her words penetrate his *aloneness* like the arrows that she bears. He holds his head and moans, but no one is listening.

And now Tefnut and Shu glide past his escorted vision, speaking of how he is a child, rather than a monster, and how one can find peace in adversity . . .yes, yes, but what about all this red!

But he pulls back when Horus appears, next, in the filmstrip. But there is no violence from the man – the human Hawk that he feared the most. And then his red right eye is streaming tears and Nephthys is standing before him and he wants to reach out to her and ask if they can still be cyborg and wife . . . and deep down the voice is laughing in what he takes to be derisory joy and he hurts so much, and it hurts, it hurts . . . to be leaking himself out into the world like this . . .

And Hathor, lovely Hathor, is holding his hand, like she did when he lay on the floor, trying to rationalize the thing they called the Mindstream. Too much, too much . . . He mumbles his apology but is spirited away by the Walker.

And now . . . and now, he is before the arc of Isis, Maat, Nut and Geb.  The place to which he flung the final arrow of Desertion at Isis, the only woman on the ship he had ever loved, if anyone could call it love. Why did he want to hurt her so much? And she speaks of turning away but she doesn't turn away from him. The eyes of power, now soft and gentle, look deeply into his world and see the tide of red.  She, alone sees it for what it is.

What is it, Isis, what is it?

"You can hurt us no longer," says Bast, echoing her brother's sentiments about empowered innocence that she and he now bear so clearly.

And now Isis is speaking about the power of higher mind to see the patterns in the swirling sand, but it is the red that was swirling, now.

He knows he has failed them all – he says so, and Isis is speaking to the pain and anguish that began when Nephthys offered herself to him.

And it is coming . . .

It is coming, as Neith binds him, with the bandages of the dead, to the Chair of Judgement. And now Isis comes to stand behind him and holds his shoulder in an act of great tenderness. But her fingers hold his head forward, and into that space come his judges, one by one, to deliver their verdicts . . . But Thoth stops them and makes them see that Setaxa should be made to judge himself . . . Am I not suffering enough? he thinks, as the coins drop on his table and he does what he needs to, and what is expected, and condemns himself with the mound of tokens in the pan. He thinks the scales of Death to be full but realises that Isis, Sekhmet and Horus hold the final pieces of his demise. But there is no change as all but Isis and Sekhmet do as the others did.

Releasing his shoulders, Isis, too, passes him her coin of judgement and now he knows there is no hope. His skin and plasteel body recoil as the Lioness curls into a kneeling position between his tied thighs. He breathes deeply, "Finish it, Sekhmet," he hears himself beg, his eyes on the laser beside her.

But she does not pick up the weapon, instead, she uncoils her right arm and delivers a slap to his face that rocks his head and changes the acoustics on the bridge of the Hawk. The silence is absolute in the wake of that lightning strike. "Let it be quick, please . . ." he can hear the child in his voice, but above that he can hear the sea of blood, Sekhmet's blood, as it rages, surging in perpetual regeneration, through channels in his body that shouldn't be there . . .

And Sekhmet is making him tell of the Captain's last message – of the words he has never understood and has been too ashamed to tell.

"That there would be a point where I had to choose death in order to live . . ." His voice is a moan, a piteous thing. There is so little of him left, now. He welcomes death and tells Sekhmet that it is so.

And then . . . and then, she is standing up and the laser is back in his hand, unused, and the woman he tortured is granting him life . . . and then the damn bursts and he is swimming in the blood of Sekhmet while they are celebrating with wine the colour of his suffering and eating bread that he knows tastes of freedom.

And somewhere in his semi-conscious state, they are giving him wine and bread, as if he could be free! But the only freedom is to go with the red flow and it gets hotter as he descends, deeper and deeper.

"I am burning," he screams.

"We know, Setaxa, You must burn, now," come the voices, in unison.

There is a fumbling at his clothes and then they are standing back amazed, at what they find. There is a mind-numbing, shocking noise, and the ship is opening up to *them* – the Mindstream, and they are coming for him, to *save* him.

But he knows it is too late, and that the *him* they are referring to is not Setaxa. And then he falls into the boiling red, the last journey of a cyborg beyond repair.

There is no pain. There is only peace. He realises that a heart, a real heart, one far stronger than any of his micro-pumps, is beating within the frame that was Setaxa. And then, he is suddenly radiant with happiness, for there, holding his dying form in his arms, is the Captain, and the Captain places a kiss on his forehead and takes his life for his own. Together now, neither of them dead, they float in a sea of Being that has changed from red to the orange and gold of the sun, awaiting the turning of the stars and the crashing of the waves on another shore.

## What's it really about?

It's really about you . . .

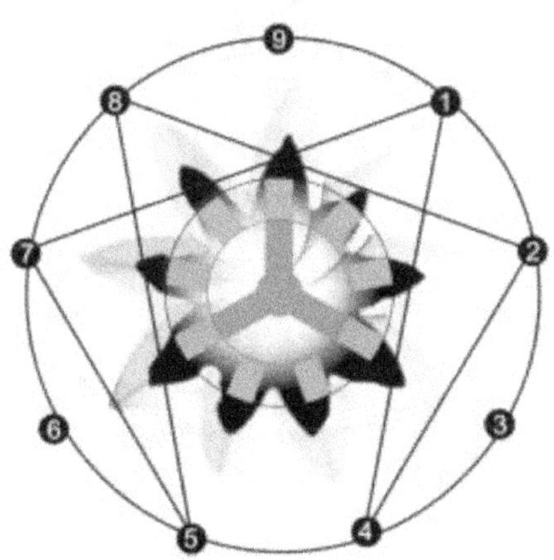

# Ritual Five
# The Blood of Sekhmet

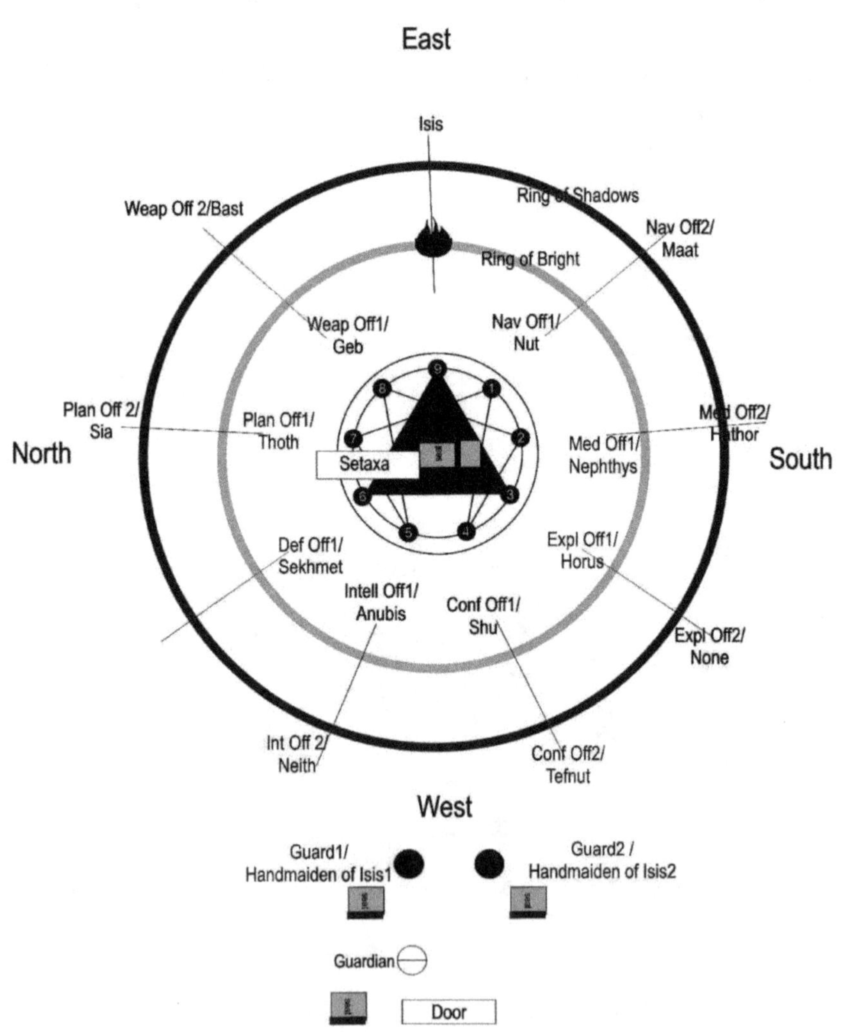

## Ritual 5 Preparation Notes

**Set up table before ritual, including:**
Laser wand.
Chair of Judgement ready to put in place of Central altar - altar moved to East
Bandages for Neith
Scales of Truth
Coins in black and white
Small table for scales
Feather of truth (held by Guardian until the end - Guardian will need table or chair for this)
Staff for Guardian
Wine goblet and red juice
Partition needs to be set up for the Handmaidens to change into the Mindstream garments
Sekhmet will need access to laser wand,
Setaxa will need access to script and scales on the table by Chair of Judgement, **with his left hand.**
Chairs for Handmaidens and Guardian - all facing East.
Music for R5

**Entry Sequence and notes for ritual:**
**Ritual R5 begins as the previous ritual.**

The Entry sequence is:
The Guardian is the first to enter. He carries out the initial consecration. The two Handmaidens of Isis enter next and take their positions to perform the Pillars of Isis.
The Guardian signals to the Technician that the entry is ready to start.
Guardian checks the entry sign of everyone.

Technician plays the entry music
<<*Music until all* (except Setaxa) *are standing in their positions*>>

Guardian gives everyone a black and white coin upon entry

The Ring of Bright enters, *clockwise*, in the order:

Shu, Horus, Nephthys, Nut, Isis, Geb, Thoth, Sekhmet, Anubis.

The Ring of Shadows enters next, *anti-clockwise*, in the order: Neith, Sia, Bast, Maat, Hathor, Tefnut.

Setaxa enters the temple but remains near the door until everyone else is ready.

When all have entered, the Technician fades out the music if still playing.

Setaxa walks forward to stand in the West.

### *Ritual Begins*

*<<Technician plays Gong>>*

**Isis**

The Mistress of Magic commands that the ritual begin. Guardian, seal this temple of Egypt!

**Guardian** *(when this is done)*
Great Isis, the Temple is sealed.

**Isis**

Handmaidens, come forward, light your lights from the flame at the centre of our temple and cense this sacred space with its light . . .
*Handmaidens (H1 and H2) enter the Ring of Bright. H1 leads a clockwise movement until both are at the East, standing before Isis, whom they salute with a short bow.*
*H2 stops there but turns to face the centre, while H1 completes the other half-circle to stop in the West, also facing the centre. When both are in that position, they walk to meet in the centre. The light their lights symbolically from the central flame, then turn, back to back, to hold the lights up facing East (H1) and West (H2).*
*Both now move synchronously, aiming to meet back at the centre at the same time.*
*H1 follows the Sekhmet moves from the previous ritual, East to the Ring of Bright, clockwise to the South, then towards the centre to meet up.*
*At the same time, H2 moves West to the Ring of Bright, clockwise to the North and inwards towards the centre to meet up with H1.*
*When they both meet up, they turn to face the East, hold up their lights and say:*

**Handmaidens** *(together, facing Isis)*
Great Isis, the temple is filled with the light from within.

**Isis**

Thank you, handmaidens.
*Handmaidens return to the West and are seated, along with the Guardian*

**Isis**

Setaxa, are you not going to join us in this last Egyptian ritual? They were staged at your request, after all?

*Setaxa walks into the middle of the temple, West of the altar, looking angry and impotent.*

**Setaxa**

I, I cannot control this, the strangeness has infected me . . . I must bring it to an end . . . my power is fading . . .

*<<Technician plays Music>>*
*Setaxa points to the laser on the Altar near the East, but stumbles to his knees on the enneagram mat, facing Isis.*

**Setaxa**

I am friendless in this place. I have exchanged a life of partnership with the Captain for a circle of enmity.

**Isis**

You had your choices, Setaxa.

**Setaxa**

What choices did I have?

**Isis** *(throws the White and Black coin to the kneeling Setaxa)*
We always have choices, even if it is only how we react to something - or even, in extremes, how we don't react at all . . . You didn't look at Horus' coin did you? It might have taught you something important.

**Setaxa** *(examines the coin, turning it over)*
It is just a coin with a black "T" on one side and a white "F" on the other?

**Nut**

Is it? Look again . . .
**Setaxa** *(studies the coin more carefully)*
Yes, you are right, I was wrong. The "T" is white on black, giving the instant impression of a black letter, if not examined carefully. The other side is the opposite, a black letter "F" on a white background - a clever optical illusion.

**Isis**

Our lives are like that, Setaxa. Yet you only saw the black letter.

**Setaxa**

The "F"? What does that mean?

**Nut**

It means you saw only our world of Fear and Falseness.

**Nephthys**

You did not look for the other, my love . . . Not even my closeness could make you turn that coin.

**Setaxa**

And what would I have found had I turned it?

**Horus**

You would have found the white letter, the "T".

**Setaxa**

And what does the "T" represent?

**Shu**

It represents Trust.
But I could not trust you! I had no guarantees that you would do what I wanted?

**Sekhmet**

Do you think our lives have guarantees in them?

**Thoth**

The wise person knows that, at any time, his or her world may change. The challenge is not the changes before us, but our reactions to them.

**Setaxa**

But I used the knowledge I took from Nephthys to show you how you have always reacted!

**Nephthys**

"Took from me" yes. But you acquired it for one purpose only!

**Geb**

You bullied Sekhmet, but you kept us all of us on our knees in the dirt, Setaxa. You looked for the base instincts in the Tribes of Mankind and you found them!

**Setaxa**

But, but . . . I looked after *you*, Isis. I gave *you* chances!

**Isis**

You were just fascinated by my moves, Setaxa, that's all. You enjoyed the challenges I presented to you . .

.

**Setaxa**

Does no-one trust me, now?

**Bast**

The Captain may have trusted you, Setaxa. Why should we?

**Maat**

You have forced obedience on us.

**Hathor**

You have reduced many of us to tears with your harshness.

**Tefnut**

Our lives hang by a thread, your loss of power may just be momentary!
*(Setaxa drops his head, shaking it)*

**Neith**

Trust is earned, Setaxa, not taken or forced. Trust is one of the universal qualities to which humans are connected, even though they don't always use it.

**Sia**

Trust requires a perception so much higher than that shared by most people. It requires that we *See* into the heart of the Universe and taste its essential goodness, unafraid of the scorn of those who say otherwise; those who will spend years proving us wrong. Truly the work of what we used to call The Devil . . .

**Bast**

Trust is gentle and silent, Setaxa. It must be found in the deepest recesses of our Selves. Once found, there is no turning back, and a new world opens . . .

**Anubis** *(comes to take Setaxa's arm, helps him rise and leads him via the outer West to his place on the Ring of Shadows, Station 6)*
Walk with me Setaxa. Walk with me through the worlds and let us show you how a Race called Mankind truly formed from the molten lava of its birth.
*(Anubis points to the ground of Station 6)*
Here was the place you chose, the place called Fear.
*(Anubis places Setaxa on his Station facing Sekhmet who turns to face him, bravely)*
*(Anubis turns to Thoth)*
Thoth, mighty in wisdom, tell us, again, of the origin of Fear.

**Thoth**

Fear is the unknown, with its potential to hurt us. It lies at the root of why we do so many things. Civilisation is our group response to fear, to the need for protection from the wild and the unpredictable. Fear makes us an island, separates us from the true world.

To live in fear is mankind's lot, and yet, on a personal level, it is also the jagged rock which forms like a molten crust, around our young selves, solidifying here, in ***the place of this tribe,*** into the fixed reaction of cowardice in the face of life's challenges - which are many. To close into habitual reaction is cowardice; to be constantly open to the good and the possible, even when these are unknown, is Courage - and Courage is the lifeblood of the flower of Osiris that strives to break through the hardened crust of the land of Fear and its people.
*(Anubis pulls Setaxa closer to Sekhmet)*

**Anubis**

Tell Setaxa, Sekhmet. Tell him about the woman he abused and why Life placed her next to him on the Ring of Bright, risking everything with her defiance.

**Sekhmet** *(with courage)*

You saw my resistance but not my courage, Setaxa. You were turned outwards. I fought for the inner, you were intent on the purpose of the outer. You had the power and so I suffered. But in that suffering my courage grew and it faces you now, hotter than the red rocks that formed the land I stand upon.

**Setaxa**

I know I wronged you, Sekhmet . . .

**Anubis**

Let us leave right and wrong for the Judgement, Setaxa. Travel with me now to the Land of Avarice.
*Anubis takes Setaxa clockwise (behind the Ring of Shadows) to Station 5 and stands him next to Neith.*
And here is the woman who could have been your wife . . .The molten lava that flowed here formed a sense of Isolation and Meanness in those who came to live in this place, they became Keepers of the Flow who hold back the streams of Life. And yet . . . tell him, Neith.

**Neith**

And yet . . . my heart opened to you in your aloneness, locked into your world of logic and pre-programmed response. I saw that in me, too, and then I could see it in everyone. You were not so bad, you were just young and frightened - and I saw that, too and offered myself to you, letting go the things and the world of isolation that had comforted me until then. You did not want me, or rather, you chose another for your own reasons of mistrust.
Through the hard and mean rock of this place grows the flower of Freedom from Attachment - and I reached down and took in its perfume. I was stronger than you, Setaxa.

**Setaxa**

Did I wrong you, Neith, with my choice?

**Anubis** *(steering Setaxa away from Neith and towards Tefnut and Shu)*
Let us leave the nature of power until the judgement, Setaxa. Here we have Tefnut and Shu, Moisture next to her elemental brother, the Air. Tefnut

confessed under your power to being the holder of Melancholy, full of Envy and uncertainty. Her tribe longs for the inner power to become what it can only long for . . .

**Tefnut** *(to Setaxa)*
You made me cry, Setaxa, with your cruelty to Sekhmet. The mists of melancholy in my soul poured out to fill the space of her suffering with balm. And yet I do not see you as a bad man, you are simply a child with absent parents, taking joy in control while he can!

**Shu** *(to Setaxa)*
You saw my sister's sadness, but not the great leap she made when you were tormenting Sekhmet. Putting her own anguish aside, she reached for the flower of Equanimity that grows through the hard rock here in the place of her tribe. Finding this peace, she could deal with you from a position of inner rather than outer power. There is no melancholy in the new Tefnut and you have created that! I should thank you!

**Setaxa**
Did I sadden your heart, Tefnut?

**Anubis** *(steering Setaxa towards Horus)*
Let us leave the nature of sadness of the heart until the Judgement, Setaxa.
Here is Horus, your epic battle with him for the soul of the Ring of Shadows shook him to his core, here in his land where the rock has hardened into Deceit. But in that battle you made him reach for the gentle flowers of honest Truth that grow in the hidden and sheltered places. And he found them, defending with each breath, this whole Land of the Exiles. And now you see that you, also, are a dweller in this land.

**Horus** *(smiling)*
You were a worthy opponent, Setaxa - and what a catalyst you have been to us all - and who could have foreseen that?

**Setaxa**
I was untruthful with you, Horus, forgive me . . .

**Anubis**

We will return to the nature of forgiveness at the Judgement, Setaxa.

*(pulls Setaxa to face Hathor and Nephthys)*

In this land the rock has hardened into little pools which fill with the water of Caring, but the water reflects back flattering images to those whose tribe inhabits them. They become full of pride. But, those who make this their home are capable of growing the flower of Humility and beyond that, of connecting with the Will of the Universe, thus becoming true servants of the Divine.

**Setaxa** *(to Nephthys)*

You gave me your love and I abused it like so much else here.

**Nephthys**

A quarrel between husband and wife should be a short affair, Setaxa. But I am also a crew member of the Hawk, and I cannot forget what you have done to them.

**Hathor**

And I am a healer, Setaxa; and made many attempts to help you. But, always they were rebutted by the mighty Cyborg and his Will - a will that humans would identify solely with the Ego!

**Setaxa**

I have used you both, badly. I have little hope of surviving your judgement of me.

**Anubis**

Your judgement is just around the corner, Setaxa. Do not try to anticipate it.

**Anubis** *(steers Setaxa to stand before Isis, Maat and Nut, and Geb)*

And so we are back at the corner of the Captain's design that deals with what you called Desertion.

**Isis**

Desertion, Setaxa - a strong word, indeed. My corner is shared with Geb and Bast to my right; and Nut and Maat to my left. I am accused of desertion and there is some truth in that, but the truth is far from the meaning you assigned to it. We of this corner are turned away, but it is the path of the Spirit from which we are turned, not the controls of a starship. The implications of the Captain's design are those of spiritual indolence not desertion.

## Geb

Under your control Bast spoke of the vengeful lust she carries against those perceived to have hurt her. But she and I fight for a return to innocence, a casting away of weapons, a recognition that the age of force and brutality is finally coming under a new lens, one of recognition that what hurts a person's soul is useless to their body.

## Bast

In this we are as one, Setaxa. You can hurt us no longer . . .

## Isis *(to Setaxa)*

Your authoritarian approach forced us to re-examine what we truly are. Being human is such a mixture of truth and error that anyone looking merely from the outside, as you did, would see only confusion. But someone of higher mind would see an ongoing process whereby the sand in the shaken bottle was gradually settling, though the path through the swirls of our lives would be invisible to the untrained eye.

## Maat

Your severity made me see my own Anger, and the relentless and often cruel search for perfection - The true flower that now grows here in the land of this Tribe will be the quest for Serenity.

## Nut

And the joy of that, the inner peace, will see a new flowering in this land, one of the recognition that Perfection is present, but it belongs only to the all-Creator whose life animates us all and in whose daily re-creation of the Eternal Mystery we all live.

We should thank you, Setaxa, for your own struggles truly concealed the other sides of the coins - the eternal truths; and therefore showed us where to search.

**Setaxa**

I have failed you all . . .

**Isis**

Failure must now be part of your Judgement. You have forced us to become something new. And in that newness we must now respond to the Strangeness that you said Nephthys had infected you with - that anguish that now burns through your brittle self like a wild fire.

**Neith** *(comes forward to face Setaxa)*

Time for the Judgement Setaxa!

*(Anubis, Neith and Nephthys bring the chair, table, scales, protective squares and laser to the centre of the temple and place the chair on the protective squares in the centre of the enneagram mat. Neith places Setaxa's script next to him on the table)*

*(Neith places the unresisting Setaxa in the chair)*

The Mistress of Weaving must secure you for your journey to Amenti.

*(Neith ties both his wrists and both ankles to the arms and legs of the chair with bandages, then places the laser wand upright in his left fist)*

**Setaxa**

I no longer care, Neith. I am unfit for this new land.

**Isis** *(comes to stand behind Setaxa's head, holding his shoulders)*

All endings are beginnings, too. Life brings Death, and Death brings Life. You know you cannot go on as you are . . . have faith.

*(looking round the temple)*

We must decide your fate. Let all come forward and place their coins on the scales to indicate the fate of Setaxa. A coin with the face of "T" means you Trust that Setaxa can have a future with us and therefore Life. A coin with the face of "F" means you Fear him and want his Death. He needs only one coin in his favour to live. That is the Law of Mercy, the reverse of the Law of Harshness.

**Anubis**

Great Isis, are we so brutalised that we have forgotten what this arrival in a new land has taught us?

**Horus**

Teach us what we have forgotten in our haste, Thoth.


**Thoth**

We who have been through so much should not mirror back that brutality. Let us therefore deliver the coins into the right hand of Setaxa, that he may judge himself . . .

Neith! Free his right hand, that he might place all the coins in the scales himself.

*(Neith unfastens the bandage from Setaxa's right hand only)*


**Isis**

That is a just gesture, Thoth. So be it! Let all deliver their coins into the left hand of Setaxa that he may decide his own fate . . .


**Isis** *(continues, holding her hands up to invoke power)*

It is time to restore the rightful order of things.

Let us begin with the Ring of Shadows, Let all come forward and cast their coins, clockwise, beginning with Bast.

*(Ring of Shadows rotates clockwise in the sequence Bast, Sia, Neith, Tefnut, Hathor, Maat, so that the active person is always at the East, that person then walks West (down the middle of the temple to the Altar) to pass in front of Setaxa and give him their coins. He places each one in either the "F" or the "T" scale with his free left hand. They then return to the East, rejoin the Ring of Shadows, and begin the Ring's rotation to the next required position. Note that this may need two spaces, so each person needs to look behind them for the "distance" to the player who follows.*


**Horus**

The Power of the Judgement must be withheld until the final moment. Isis, Sekhmet and I will do this, let the rest of those in the Ring of Bright now rotate the Ring and cast their coins.

*(Ring of Bright also rotates clockwise in the sequence Geb, Thoth, Anubis, Shu, Nephthys, Nut, so that the active person is always at the East, that person then walks West (down the middle of the temple to the Altar) to pass in front of Setaxa and give him their coins. He places each one in either the "F" or the "T" scale with his free right hand. They then return to the East, rejoin the Ring of Bright, and begin the Ring's rotation to the next*

*required position. Note that this may need two spaces, so each person needs to look behind them for the "distance" to the player who follows)*
*(When all the above have cast their coins, Setaxa nods his head, sadly, knowing his fate)*

**Setaxa**
It is just. I deserve to die and you have granted me the freedom to condemn myself, at least.
*(Finally, Isis and Horus give their coins to Setaxa's right hand. then return to their former positions. Isis continues to hold Setaxa's shoulders)*

**Setaxa** *(looking back up at her)*
You do as they do, Isis? Then my last hope is gone . . .

**Isis**
Then let hope change to something else, Setaxa.
*(Setaxa stares at Sekhmet who approaches him, cat-like, for the kill)*

**Setaxa**
Finish it, Sekhmet . . . the laser wand is yours . . .
*(Sekhmet curls into a kneeling position between Sekhmet's bound legs. She fingers her coin in her left hand and stares into his eyes, then slaps him across the face with her right hand. He reels with the blow, but says nothing)*

**Sekhmet**
So much suffering, so much humiliation. You deserve to die, you monster!

**Setaxa (***nods his head)*
I do, brave Lioness. Let it be quick, please . . .
*(Sekhmet takes the laser wand out of Setaxa's left hand and places its tip on the centre of his forehead)*

**Sekhmet**
Before you die, tell us about the Captain's last instruction - the one you had so much trouble with?

**Setaxa** *(softly)*
He said there would come a point where I had to choose death in order to

live. Now that prophecy is coming true in a way that no chess-player could have foreseen.

**Sekhmet**

And did you understand it when he said it?

**Setaxa**

No.

**Sekhmet**

And do you understand it now?

**Setaxa**

No . . . there is no logic to it, and yet I feel its solution lies just behind my eyes . . . but I cannot grasp it. *(hangs his head)* Finish it Sekhmet. I am tired of living my life this way . . .

**Sekhmet** *(puts the laser back into his left hand and holds her coin before his eyes)*
Then what do **you** choose?

**Setaxa**

I choose death.

**Sekhmet**

Why do you choose something you do not yet understand?

**Setaxa**

Because the Captain said it and I have always been true to him, if not to others . .

**Sekhmet** *(stands, looking down at Setaxa)*
Then the judgement is ended. You have earned your life through your Faith, and we honour the memory of the Captain more than anything else . . .
*(she turns to place the coin on the other side of the scales with the "T" symbol upwards. She lets Setaxa look in amazement then pushes down the "T" side of the scales with her hand, scattering all the coins.)*

There is an old temple saying, Setaxa, that there is not enough darkness in the whole Universe to put out the light of a single candle . . . Remember this single candle all your days!

**Isis**
Let us have a celebration of inner life. Sia, Hathor, bring us the bread and the wine.
*(Sia and Hathor distribute bread and wine to all.)*

**Isis**
The grapes of my body can only become wine after the wine-maker has trampled me. I surrender my spirit like grapes to his trampling so my inner-most heart can blaze and dance with joy.
Companions, raise your glasses in a toast to Life.
*(All say, "to Life".)*
*Isis gives the still-bound Setaxa some bread and wine, then puts his glass on the side table)*
<<Technician plays Mindstream >>
*(Handmaidens go quietly behind the screen to put on the Mindstream tabards, then come to stand in their normal positions, but facing East)*

**Setaxa** *(writhes his upper body)*
I am burning, Isis!

**Sekhmet**
We know, Setaxa. You must burn, now.

**Setaxa**
My blood is on fire, Horus - I am a burning! Help me!

**Sekhmet**
The flames must grow higher yet, Setaxa . . .

**Setaxa** *(screaming)*
Sekhmet, I am dying! The heat - help me!
*(Sekhmet reaches to open the zip of Setaxa's jacket and pushes it off his body. The blood red outline of a heart is revealed, dripping in its birth struggle. Sekhmet stands back in amazement, staring at the act of creation unfolding before her)*

**The Guardian** *strikes his staff three times. loudly.*
*<<Technician plays Mindstream, then immediately, >>*


**Anubis** *(closes his eyes, attuning to the Mindstream)*
They are here . . . *(goes directly to the West and symbolically opens the Ship's doors, bowing to the twins of the Mindstream)*
*(Anubis escorts the Mindstream twins directly up the middle line from the West towards the centre. They stop halfway to Setaxa's chair.)*


**Mindstream twins** *(speaking together)*
We were called. We have answered that call. There is urgency.
*(pointing to Setaxa)* That one is failing. His was the voice that called to us.


**Isis**
He is in pain but he did not call!


**Mindstream twins** *(together)*
Not his outer, his inner, the one you call Captain, the one who called to us when the ship came into our planet's orbit, to say that his life was fading and that he had only one chance to live . . .


**Horus**
The Captain placed himself into Setaxa?


**Mindstream Twins** *(together)*
Yes, it is a miracle of what you would call bio-engineering, but his life-force survives now as a child, within the machinery of the Cyborg. In this manner, he is being re-born or more accurately, twin-born. The outer will remain, linked to his newly developing mind, as servant to master . . .


**Anubis**
But his rebirth pains have drained what little strength remained. I can see through your eyes and sense that! Can you save him?


**Mindstream Twins** *(together)*
Not without blood.

**Isis**

You can have whatever blood you need from any of us. Save him, please!

**Mindstream Twins** *(together)*

It must be blood from his own family. We can enrich it, but the source must be familial.

**Sekhmet**

I . . . I can provide it!

**Setaxa** *(very weakly)*

You . . . Sekhmet. But you are not related to me?

**Sekhmet**

Not to the tyrant Setaxa, but, beyond these roles you made us play, I am the Captain's sister. That was the knowledge that I didn't want you to have because you would have abused it!

**Setaxa**

And you would now give your blood to save me?

**Sekhmet**

No, Setaxa, I would give my blood to save what you are becoming . . . *(turns to the Mindstream Twins and offers her heart area to them)*
I will gladly give what you need.

**Mindstream twins** *(together)*

We only need a little. The natural forces of the planet you call Idos will do the rest.
*(The Mindstream twins pick up Setaxa's goblet from the table and hold it to the heart of Sekhmet, then they raise it to the East in salutation, and carry it to the lips of Setaxa, who drinks it all (don't worry if some spills it will add to the effect). When he has drunk it all, Setaxa falls asleep.)*

**Mindstream twins** *(together)*

Your Captain will be as a child. You must raise and nurture him. The once great man may return, but that is in your hands, alone. We cannot interfere further.

*(they move back to the West, collecting the Feather of Truth from the Guardian, They turn and face the East and say, together:*

You are renewed. You are welcome on Idos. Bring only peace and hold love in your hearts, always. Know that there is only one Truth, but there are many windows upon its light. Grow tolerance in your hearts and respect them all, for each traveller must have their personal journey.

*(Mindstream twins take the Feather of Truth from the Guardian and let it fall to the floor in the West of the Temple.*

By this weight you will be measured.

*(Mindstream twins bow to the East, then bow to the Guardian, then leave the temple – please keep quiet in the corridor while the ritual ends)*

**Isis**

Sekhmet, you have saved us all, my heart thanks you with joy. We must guard and nurture our re-born Captain, our own Osiris. Please go to the East and close our sacred rite. A play it may have been but it has served us so very well!

**Sekhmet** *(goes to East, holds up her hands in a symbol of collecting Royal power from the Sun, then faces West)*

Beloved Companions, we shall now close our rite. It is time to go out into the world of Idos. What we find there depends on *how we See*. Let us hold in our hearts this time together and cherish its memories and the flowers that grow from the seeds of its experience in the soil of our lives.

**Sekhmet** *(continues)*

Guardian, please unseal our temple. We thank you for your diligent work in making this space safe and sacred.

*(Guardian unseals the temple, bows to the East)*

**Guardian**

The temple is unsealed, Sekhmet. You may now leave this sacred space with love in your hearts.

**Sekhmet**

Companions, please face the East and play your right hands over your heart.

Say together: "In the Light and the Truth, in the Garden of Maat"
*(all do so)*
Companions, please face the West and bow to honour the Guardian and the Handmaidens of Isis.
*(all do so)*
The worlds of Bright and Shadow are healed into the single Ring that they always were, when seen from the centre. Let us symbolise that by both rings leaving together, clockwise. Because we have carried out a group salutation, no further temple actions are necessary. Please leave from the West two by two.
It is ended. Let us leave and take up our lives in the world, again.

*Sekhmet leaves directly down the centre of the Temple on an East-West line.*
*Technician plays:*
*<< Gong, then music …leave playing until all have left the temple>>*
*Both Rings leave together, clockwise, doubling up at the West and walking out in pairs.*
*Upholders and Technician leave the temple, clockwise.*
*The Guardian remains in the West.*
*Isis, Horus and Anubis remain in the temple, forming a protective ring around the new child. When all but the Guardian have left, they wait a few moments then depart to join the Companions. The Guardian leaves with them.*

*Please maintain silence until the last person has left the temple.*

### The Land of the Exiles
*11 March 2014.*

# Adventure into Being

**Jordis Fasheh**
*Nephthys*

The journey into being continued from our last gathering in the Derbyshire hills after a rich and tumultuous year of transformation exploring the unknown of speaking from my soul and learning to listen to my inner wisdom. I was filled with expectation, excitement and longing for the companionship of soul mates who share a similar love for diving deep into the heart of the one through ritual and play.

I prepared for the long trip across the sea from California to England. Read through the script and prepared for the role of Nephthys, and while breathing in the creativity of ancient wisdom, I packed my things and headed off. Of course, the journey is always present and as I left my apartment, the church bells rang to ring in the day. I walked out of my apartment and as I was locking the front door, I noticed a feather on the floor just outside lying there as the first sign of what would awaken inside of me as I acted the part of Nephthys and I knew then that I would return with a full heart and an even deeper love of the unknown where creation lives and anything is possible.

I met up with Benjamin, a companion of the Silent Eye who lives in Salem, Oregon and we set off together. We talked, laughed and shared our inner thoughts, fears and hopes. We had a lot in common and got to explore Somerset for several days before the weekend with the companions. It was wonderful finding great Pubs, old churches, meeting new people and soaking in the culture of England.

We hooked up with Alienora on Friday morning and headed off for the long drive to Derbyshire and the Nightingale Centre to meet up with Steve, Sue, Stuart and the companions. The three of us got to bond on the drive up and talked about what we would bring to our quest and what we wanted to shed and open up the space needed to soak in the lessons. We had common challenges and it was healing to realize that you were not alone on this journey and had friends that would walk with you on the path to enlightenment.

It was wonderful to meet up with everyone on Friday; companions from our last weekend together and new souls who chose to embark on the journey with us. Of course, the weekend was packed with lectures, ritual preparation, food, laughter, and good times.

I spent a lot of time rehearsing my lines and being Nephthys, I completely related to her character and recognized that Steve, Sue and Stuart knew us well enough to know what we would need to grow. Nephthys had a mysterious quality and while she never had children, she was the Mother of Anubis, the transporter of soul's to the other-side. I had recently experienced the dying process of my dear Aunt Fadwa and held vigil with her and my cousin Sylvia until her passing. At one point, she asked me if it was my responsibility to stay with the dying. And of course, I answered yes. She was completely selfless in life and in death and was more concerned with my well being than her own. It was great because I could get her to go to sleep if I said that I would sleep next to her. In her death, she taught me what love is and that conflict arises when we can only see our reflection in the mirror, when we miss the other's beingness. The role of Nephthys allowed me to dive deeper into my soul, hear its voice loud and clear and know who I really am, the One, I Am. Blessed be.

The problem was with the costume, I was so busy at work and did not have the time to prepare proper attire for my role. I thought that I could find a robe, a feather and ornaments in Glastonbury. But alas nothing seemed to be suitable and I kicked myself for not bringing along the feather that I found outside my doorstep. But it all worked out, Alienora had a wonderful purple robe that I wore over my white robe and I was able to find a feather with two skulls on it that I wore in my hair.

Before the journey, I was torn, my soul yearning to be free yet feeling bereft at times, not able to pull myself out of the life I had been living. What I perceived as obligations, widowed Father, job, bills, etc. was a huge weight on my shoulders. It was Friday night at the Pub after our first ritual that I braved the storm and decided to have a conversation about these feelings with Steve. He began speaking of the undertoad from John Irving's "World According to Garp." The undertoad as the Superego pulls you under every time you seem to be pulling ahead. I understood that the feeling of bereftness was that undertoad disguised as guilt and obligation and was holding me back from truly allowing my soul to be in the driver's seat. I felt so at ease and allowed the emotions to swirl and float away. I loved how lighthearted Steve was and how he brought forth transformation through play and with his wisdom was able to help disperse a lifetime of anguish. Of course, I chose to let it go and it was immediate at the moment but took the weekend and next few months to unfold.

Actually, the entire weekend evolved in this manner, Steve as Setaxa, Osiris masked as a cyborg, tormenting everyone, especially Sekhmet with his laser gun. The rituals were colourful, creative and went deep. The cast wore fabulous costumes, Sue as Isis with her beautifully embroidered flowing robe with wings, Stuart as Anubis wearing a mask that would shock and amaze the personality out of the present, Ali as Sekhmet in a gorgeous blood red robe with a lionesses face and of course Debora wearing an authentic robe from Dubai was as alluring as the full moon at midnight.

But the best, was during our early morning ritual and climb up to the hillside, when after a quiet walk up the hill with the companions at 6:00 am, we witnessed Steve as Osiris fully bound with the rope that Sue and Stuart so happily tightly wrapped around him. There Osiris stood, bound, completely silent for the entire ritual as we spoke our words of truth and walked through the gateway that Isis and Anubis so patiently held open as we consciously and lovingly went through to the other side. The side of truth, creation, love, expression and the sacred.

Alas the weekend was splendid, eyes wide open, but it was time to depart, and with a heavy heart, knowing it would be yet another year before I could be with the companions again. However, also knowing that we would be in constant communication, as companions with lessons and growth during the entire time away from each other.

As I write this letter, my heart is full of love and gratitude for the companionship of all the souls that choose to travel together along an ancient path toward our ancestral home. Blessed be.

# This sparkling of the soul

**Debora Zachariasse**
*Nut*

It was the first time in 53 years (cryo-time not included) that I actually crashed on an alien planet.

In retrospect, I should have been alerted as we headed off, that something special was up. Our ship had the best crew I had seen for many journeys. Surely that was no coincidence.

But for sheer joy of meeting my fellow travellers, I hadn't allowed my cynicism and suspicion take their natural course to teach me some lonely wisdom. Instead, I was a fool and I let joy reign my heart.

Many of this crew had become good friends over years of space-time drudgery. So I went in to cryo quite unsuspecting, letting myself slide slowly into that cold oblivion that I had come to know so well. Surely the Captain knew what he was doing. I had worked with him through three long journeys and I not only respected him as a wise leader, but also as a well loved friend.

Spacecraft are amazingly silent. No beeps, no clinks, none of the clattering or vrooming the comic book writers want you to believe. Any sounds are more like the soothing humming of the honeybees. Which, of course, is another excellent induction to sleep.

So the awakening was rough. Physically, we were alright, though in shock from the crash, but the worst bit was that our captain had disappeared. In his place we were stuck with a merciless machine who showed great cruelty to one of our crewmembers. By holding her hostage, he drove us into submission and set us these impossible tasks, impersonating the very Creator Gods of ancient Egypt just for a spectator sport. As if.

We were bound to this devilish plot, for we loved our fellow officer well and we didn't want to see her hurt. So we gave it our best. It was then that the dreams started.

Dreams about an Earth life. I was living in a watery country filled with rivers and marshes, lush meadows and cloud-heavy skies amidst flowers and honeybees. It was a paradise. Surely it must have been the incessant humming that brought images like that to my mind. My dreams portrayed many of these same people I knew so well from traveling across the universe together. They blended in as friends, lovers even, from another life, a life in which we were all studying together, enjoying nature together, delving deeply into the currents of time and space and learning a strange, theatrical and yet deeply moving art form we called magic.

It seemed, in this dream life, that some intriguing form of natural cohesion took place, drawing us toward each other by resonance-identification, causing unlikely friendships to blossom. Information was exchanged almost without realizing it. Unfortunately, this cohesive process was impervious to practicalities like time and space, so members of my resonance-group were scattered across the globe, living in the Netherlands, the US, England, Scotland, Gabon, Italy, Dubai or even as far as Australia. It was obvious that this natural cohesion mattered a lot, since the Creators of Coincidence went through such an incredible amount of trouble to bring us together.

Whenever we met, it set the soul on fire, the sparks shooting off in all directions.

It was a contagious thing, this sparkling of the soul.

So maybe this geological isolation was for a very good reason after all. Those watery dreams certainly added urgency to our impossible mission. Thanks to our First Officer, we managed to tame the machine and let him regurgitate the Captain that he had cruelly devoured - the only way, as it turned out, to keep him alive, for we were on a heavy duty mission and it took heavy duty payment off our Captain. Letting himself be absorbed by the machine was the only way he saw to stay alive.

He, too, had dreamed, and none too pleasantly. In his dream he had stood guard, frozen on a hillside, green with anxiety and unable to move, yet handing out Life force to all who bowed down to him. But in that illogical way of the land of dreams, it seemed to be the only way. Fortunately, our First Officer was non relenting and ingenious and we found our Captain in time, alive and kicking. We quickly dismantled the wretched computer and saved the useful bits, repaired the ship and now we're ready for new adventures. But in all my career, this was the strangest one as yet.

Already I detect the faintest noise, a mere humming, like the honeybees silently singing to the Sun, and I know the ship is ready for take-off to new and unexpected places. Who knows one day we will wake up on a new planet, and find us in that watery little paradise that haunted my dreams...

# About the author: Steve is

a well-known figure in the esoteric world and has been a keynote presenter at many conferences and workshops. Born into a Rosicrucian family in Bolton, Lancashire, in 1954, Steve grew up surrounded by mystical discussion and fascinating but often peculiar grown-ups. In adult life, and alongside a career in IT, he became an officer and then the Lodge Master of AMORC's John Dalton Chapter in Manchester. After having a decade off to help raise their two boys through the early stage of their lives, he returned to active mystical service and was soon asked to take a field officer role with the Rosicrucian Order, AMORC. This began an intensive seven year period of service culminating in the role of Grand Councillor for the North of England, Scotland and Ireland.

Steve retired from AMORC in 2005 with full military honours and fond memories of some wonderful times shared, including a final initiation in the King's Chamber of the Great Pyramid of Gizeh - something not easily bettered!

Shortly after, he met Dolores Ashcroft-Nowicki, Director of Studies of the Servants of the Light School, and her husband Michael, then in charge of all the back-office systems for SOL. It was a prophetic meeting as Steve was, shortly thereafter, to create SOL's computerised administration systems for Dolores and Michael, set up a SOL Lodge in Manchester, and become a founding member of the ARC Administration team to establish SOL's online presence and offer the lessons to a world-wide audience via the internet and electronic payment systems. Part of this undertaking was to be invited into SOL's House of the Amethyst and take the SOL highest initiation - the Third Degree - Adept.

Steve is the Founding Director of the Silent Eye, a modern Mystery School, along with Sue Vincent and Stuart France.

Steve publishes a daily blog at http://lakesteve.blogspot.co.uk/ where confusion, humour and occasional teaching may be found.

**Stuart France** – 'lunatic', writer and mystic, possibly in that order. Stuart has a deep and practical knowledge of the Western Mystery Tradition, having followed a Path that has taken him hopping through the branches of the Trees of Knowledge and Delight. His astonishing work with symbolism and the interpretation of myth comes from a profound understanding and love of life, humanity and fine

cheese! After gaining his BA in Philosophy and Literature, and his MA in Writing, this Child of Light studied with OBOD, AMORC, and the Servants of the Light and is a Director of The Silent Eye School of Consciousness. He declines all responsibility for this introduction. *"I blame Wen….."*

**Sue Vincent** is a Yorkshire born writer, esoteric teacher and Director of The Silent Eye. She has been immersed in the Mysteries all her life. Sue maintains a popular blog *Daily Echo* at **www.scvincent.com** and is co-author of *The Mystical Hexagram* with Dr G.M.Vasey. Sue lives in Buckinghamshire, having been stranded there some years ago due to an accident with a blindfold, a pin and a map. She has a lasting love-affair with the landscape of Albion, the hidden country of the heart. She is currently owned by a small dog who also blogs.

The friendship of Vincent and France has a peculiar alchemy of humour, scholarship and vision that has given birth to several books, including *The Initiate, Heart of Albion* and *Giants Dance*.

The Silent Eye School of Consciousness is a modern Mystery School that seeks to allow its students to find the inherent magic in living and being. With students around the world the School offers a fully supervised and practical correspondence course that explores the self through guided inner journeys and daily exercises. It also offers workshops that combine sacred drama, lectures and informal gatherings to bring the teachings to life in a vivid and exciting format. The Silent Eye operates on a not-for-profit basis. Full details of the School may be found on the official website, where there is also a forum open to all: **www.thesilenteye.co.uk**

# THE INITIATE:

## Adventures in Sacred Chromatography

## Sue Vincent & Stuart France

*Foreword by Steve Tanham*

Imagine wandering through an ancient landscape wrought in earth and stone, exploring the sacred sites of peoples long ago and far away in time and history. The mounds and barrows whisper legends of heroes and magic, painted walls sing of saints and miracles and vision seeps through the cracks of consciousness.

Now imagine that the lens of the camera captures a magical light in soft blues and misty greens and gold. A light that seems to have no cause in physical reality. What would you do?

If you were open to the possibility of deeper realities, perhaps you would wish to explore this strange phenomenon...something two people came to know as sacred chromatography.

The Initiate is the story of just such a journey beyond the realms of our accustomed normality. It is a factual tale told in a fictional manner. In this way did the Bards of old hide in the legends and deeds of heroes those deeper truths for those who had eyes to see and ears to hear.

As the veils thin and waver, time shifts and the present is peopled with the shadowy figures of the past, weaving their tales through a quest for understanding and opening wide the doors of perception for those who seek to see beyond the surface of reality.

*"..this is a work of Art and it is very definitely unique." Dr G.M.Vasey, author of "The Last Observer" and "Inner Journeys: Explorations of the Soul"*

*"Although a very mature, serious and in many ways learned study and in no way to imply a simplistic form, there is also about it the originality, freshness, zest and sheer joie de vivre of some of the much beloved adventure stories of my childhood – an irresistible and all too rare combination." B. Terrier*

Over 60 Full Colour Illustrations

# THE HEART OF ALBION:

## Tales from the Wondrous Head

## Stuart France & Sue Vincent

*"If I am consciously following a woman who is about to engage a Llama in conversation, which I certainly appear to be, it does not impinge too negatively upon my thought processes."*

What does Jack and the Beanstalk have to do with a spiritual quest? What, for that matter, is the nature of the relationship between Salome and the Jester? Why is Wen conversing with a llama in the Yorkshire Dales? And what links the beautiful and sacred landscape that is the Heart of Albion with Breakfast in Slug Town? These, and many other questions, must be considered as Don and Wen continue the journey begun in The Initiate exploring the shadowy roots of the ancient myths and legends of these Blessed Isles, steering a perilous path through the murky waters of religious symbolism and iconography.

*"Breakfast in Slug Town?"*

Join them on their continuing quest for knowledge and understanding as they explore the landscape of England and people it with strange creatures and even stranger theories, using sacred intent and guided imagination to penetrate into the mysteries unfolding before them.

Illustrated in full colour throughout

# GIANTS DANCE:
## Rhyme and Reason

## Stuart France and Sue Vincent

It began with a walk over the bracken covered hillsides of Derbyshire to a lonely stone circle, almost forgotten. It was just a walk...until the hawk flew from the tree and once again the visions began.

Plunged into a realm beyond reality, further than history, deeper than time, Don and Wen begin to unravel the hidden messages hidden in plain sight, concealed by habit and acceptance, and extraordinary magic framed within the small things of ordinary life.

Follow a journey across the Heart of Albion and become an Initiate of the mysterious verity of verse.

*"Interesting that they should seek to make the seven four like that."*
*"Three harmonic pairs and a jubilant head?"*
*"It reminds me of something biblical."*
*"It wouldn't be Jubilees would it? The Hebrews, you know, took an awful lot with them when they fled from Egypt."*
*"I know, but it's not Jubilees, although that does bear some consideration. It's the three-score years and ten! It's precisely the same dynamic. In fact, we even raised the question of whether there was anything in the tradition appertaining to it."*
*"And now we have our answer!"*
*"The Hebrew's Divinely sanctioned earthly span of life is determined by the Seven Hathors."*

Illustrated in Full Colour throughout

# SWORD OF DESTINY

## Sue Vincent

*"…and the swords must be found and held by their bearers lest the darkness find a way into the heart of man. Ask the waters to grant guidance and tell the ancient Keeper of Light that it is time to join battle for the next age."*

Rhea Marchant heads north to the wild and beautiful landscapes of the Yorkshire Dales where she is plunged into an adventure that will span the worlds. The earth beneath her feet reveals its hidden life as she and her companions are guided by the ancient Keeper of Light in search of artefacts of arcane power. With the aid of the Old Ones and the merry immortal Heilyn, the company seek the elemental weapons that will help restore hope to an unbalanced world at the dawn of a new era.

" Sue writes with a real grasp of the human side of people which is expressed in the personalities of her heroes and the recognizable characters that they interact with. The power and essence of her story is found in the admixture of her undoubted love of Yorkshire, her ability to see the warm and the good in all people, and her knowledge of the magical forces one can find at work in such places and between such folk. An inspired piece of writing that keeps your attention until the very last page." *Dr G.M.Vasey, author of "The Last Observer" and "Inner Journeys: Explorations of the Soul ", co-author of "The Mystical Hexagram: The Seven Inner Stars of Power".*

# THE LIVING ONE:

## Contemplations on the Gospel of Thomas

## Stuart France

*"...It is like the smallest of seeds and if it falls on prepared soil, it produces the largest of plants and shelters the birds of heaven..."*

Many scholars believe that the Gospel According to Thomas preserves a glimpse into the oral traditions of the Gospels. The book is a collection of sayings, parables and dialogues attributed to Jesus and forms part of the Nag Hammadi Library, a collection of ancient papyri found near the Dead Sea in 1945.

In this unique interpretation Stuart France brings the oral tradition to life, retelling the Gospel in his own words, in the way it may have been shared around the hearthfires of our forefathers. Deeply entwined with the story is the personal journey to understanding, following it down some rather unusual pathways. It begins with a road trip in an arid landscape far from home; a journey that led through a country that captured imagination and set it to music. It ends with an ancient story, told as you have never read it before.

*"Look, it's obvious, mozzies are God's Angels in disguise."*

Accompanied by a commentary which draws upon the esoteric traditions of the Mystery Schools, The Living One provides a new window on an age old story, being a transmutation of the spirit of the words, born of the personal realisations of a seeker after Truth.

*"Salome said to Joshua, "Who are you mister, you have eaten from my table and climbed on to my couch as if you are a stranger ?""*

"a fascinating and unique look at this important Gospel," *Dr G.M.Vasey, author of "The Last Observer" and "Inner Journeys: Explorations of the Soul",*

# CRUCIBLE OF THE SUN:

## The Mabinogion Retold

## By Stuart France

*"I will dazzle like fire, hard and high, will flame the breaths of my desire; chief revealer of that which is uttered and that which is asked, tonight I make naked the word."*

Once upon a time we gathered around the flames of the hearth and listened to tales of long ago and far away. The stories grew in the telling, weaving ancient lore whose origins lie somewhere in a misty past with tales of high adventure, battles, magic and love. In Crucible of the Sun this oral tradition is echoed in a unique and lyrical interpretation of tales from the Mabinogion, a collection of stories whose roots reach back into the depths of time, spanning the world and reflecting universal themes of myth and legend.

These tales capture a narrative deeply entwined through the history of the Celtic peoples of the British Isles, drawing on roots that are embedded in the heart of the land. In Crucible of the Sun the author retells these timeless stories in his own inimitable and eminently readable style. The author's deep exploration of the human condition and the transitions between the inner worlds illuminate this retelling, casting a unique light on the symbolism hidden beyond the words, unravelling the complex skein of imagery and weaving a rich tapestry of magic.

*'The author's creative and scholarly engagement with the material and enthusiasm for the original tales is evident throughout.' The Welsh Books Council*

*'I found it very inspiring!' Philip Carr-Gomm, Chosen Chief, Order of Bards, Ovates and Druids (O.B.O.D.)*

# THE MYSTICAL HEXAGRAM:

## The Seven Inner Stars of Power

## Dr G. Michael Vasey & S.C.Vincent

*Foreword by Dolores Ashcroft-Nowicki*

The Mystical Hexagram is a new book by Dr G. Michael Vasey and S.C.Vincent. The book explores a symbol. Not from some scholarly or deeply complex perspective, but seeing it as a representation relating to life and living. The forces and pressures that are associated with the hexagram are, after all the forces of life at both practical and Universal levels. By exploring and beginning to understand the symbol, we are able to learn and discover more about ourselves.

The meditations throughout the book take you on an inner journey of exploration, discovering the parallels between the self and the greater reality within which we live our lives. They illustrate the connection between the inner and outer world of the self and the cosmic forces of Creation. Having traced that connecting path, the meditations offer a practical way of applying that understanding.

In addition to the exercises the book includes two very special meditations, The Garden of Remembrance and the Circle of Healing. These two you will want to revisit many times, taking away from the experience a sense of peace and beauty.

*"Above all The Mystical Hexagram is intended to be a magical guide, one that is a solid contribution to the genre." Gordon Strong, author of The Five Tarots, Lion of Light and many other books.*

*"The combination of the authors' writing skills, S.C. Vincent's artistic talent and their wonderful visionary abilities make this a fascinating and thought-provoking read." Alienora Taylor, author of Long Leggety Beasties*

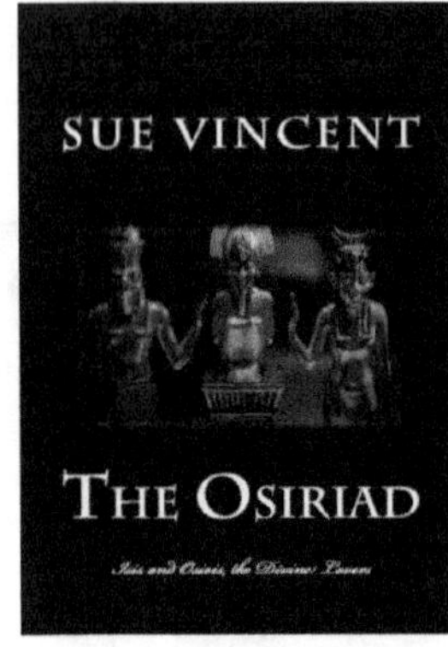

# THE OSIRIAD
## Isis & Osiris, the Divine Lovers

## Sue Vincent

*"There was a time we did not walk the earth. A time when our nascent essence flowed, undifferentiated, in the Source of Being."*

In forgotten ages, the stories tell, the gods lived and ruled amongst men. Many tales were told, across many times and cultures, following the themes common to all mankind. Stories were woven of love and loss, magic and mystery, life and death. One such story has survived from the most distant times. In the Two Lands of Ancient Egypt a mythical history has been preserved across millennia. It begins with the dawn of Creation itself and spans one of the greatest stories ever to capture the heart and imagination. Myths are, by their very nature, organic. They grow from a seed sown around a hearthfire, perhaps, and the stories travelled the ancient highways, embellished and adapted with each retelling. Who knows what the first story told? In this retelling of the ancient story it is the Mistress of all Magic herself who tells the tale of the sacred family of Egypt.

"We have borne many names and many faces, my family and I. All races have called us after their own fashion and we live their stories for them, bringing to life the Universal Laws and Man's own innermost heart. We have laughed and loved, taught and suffered, sharing the emotions that give richness to life. But for now, I will share a chapter of my family's story. One that has survived intact through the millennia, known and remembered still, across your world. Carved in stone, written on papyrus, I will tell you of a time when my name was Isis."

*"..a gifted story-teller, and her knowledge of ancient lore, as well as the ancient, eternal wisdom of "Truth," is apparent in this book. " Alethea Kehas, Inner Truth Healing*

# NOTES FROM A SMALL DOG

## Four Legs on Two

## Sue Vincent

"He asked me what it is with balls…why I love them so much. I had a think about that. It is 'cause they fly. Like birds. I'm supposed to chase birds. I'm a bird-dog. 'Course, she won't really let me. It doesn't stop me barking at 'em and seeing 'em off from my garden. But it isn't the same. Somewhere, deep inside, I know what I am supposed to do, what I am supposed to be. But I can't be that for some reason… things aren't quite set up right for me to chase birds all day and bring them back to her. On the other hand, that's who I am…and you can't be anything else than that… so the balls let me be myself in a world where I can't catch birds all day. She says that's not unusual… She seems to think that we all know who we really are, deep down, and that we spend all our time trying to find a way to be that in a world that doesn't quite seem to fit. We either find other stuff to express it…like balls…. Or we try and be what others think we should be… But you can't be a terrier if you are a retriever, can you? A bit like asking a fish to climb trees. It can be done, but it isn't easy!"

Ani, a very familiar spirit, was named for one of the ancient gods. It should, I suppose, have been no surprise when she took over the keyboard and began to write. A year later she had me collect her writings into a single volume at the insistence of her fans… who have been taken by her playful love of life and her odd wisdom…largely because she is saving for an automatic tennis ball launcher.. She even lets me write occasionally… By this time you may, of course, think I am barking mad myself… you may have a point… but I stand with Orhan Pamuk, "Dogs do speak, but only to those who know how to listen."

*"I don't know how you could read this and not fall in love."* Rosie Amber, author of *Talk of the Playground.*

# THE SONG OF THE TROUBADOUR:

## A Silent Eye Workbook

## by Steve Tanham

*Foreword by Sue Vincent*

*With contributions from Stuart France and those who were there to share this very special journey.*

"Being is without beginning and end. This flowing, loving, intelligence is the basis of everything we know. Whatever level of consciousness we attain, it will only reveal the greater and greater depth of Being that has always been there within us and before us.

Being also forms the objects that we believe are separated from us. But the Reality and the Truth are that we live and have our own being in a sea of endless loving energy that is our true home. There is no separation, there is in the end, no journey; there is only realisation, and seeing. What unveils itself before us, was always there."

A group of pilgrims have been brought together in the ancient monastery of the Keepers of the First Flame. Unexpectedly, the door opens and into their midst stride the Troubadours, holding a Child by the hand…. a very special Child in whom the Light of Being shines clear… and who can see the world as it really is. The Troubadours are on an urgent mission to save the life of a King and they enlist the aid of the pilgrims to care for the Child as they fathom the meaning an ancient and prophetic riddle….

Thus began the inaugural weekend that saw the Birthing of the Silent Eye, a modern Mystery School. This workbook is both a practical transcript of the dramatic rituals of that weekend and the story of that Birth. The book opens a window onto the workings of a modern Mystery school, sharing the accounts of some of those who attended the weekend as well as the detailed script of the powerful ritual drama. If you have ever wondered what really goes on… this book is for you.

# DOOMSDAY: THEÆTHELING THING

## Stuart France & Sue Vincent

*"Who was this Arviragus bloke anyway?"*
Don studies the light as it plays through his beer, casting prisms on the table. How is it possible to hide such a story... the hidden history of Christianity in Britain? Oh, there are legends of course... old tales... Yet what if there was truth in them? What was it that gave these blessed isles such a special place in the minds of our forefathers? There are some things you are not taught in Sunday School. From the stone circles of the north to the Isle of Avalon, Don and Wen follow the breadcrumbs of history and forgotten lore to uncover a secret veiled in plain sight.

*Wen is checking something in the Dictionary, "Get this... 'ætheling from O.E. .Æpling, 'son of a king, man of royal blood, nobleman, chief, prince, king, Christ, God-Man, Hero, Saint...'*

*"Wait a minute... wait a minute... give me that last bit again."*

*"...Christ, God-Man, Hero, Saint..."*

*"Didn't we call our Arthur, Aeth in, 'The Heart of Albion'?"*

Illustrated in full colour throughout